D1452780

Indoctrination and Education

STUDENTS LIBRARY OF EDUCATION

Indoctrination and Education

I. A. Snook

Department of Education,
University of Canterbury,
Christchurch, New Zealand

LONDON AND BOSTON
ROUTLEDGE & KEGAN PAUL

First published 1972
by Routledge & Kegan Paul Ltd
Broadway House, 68-74 Carter Lane,
London EC4V 5EL and
9 Park Street,
Boston, Mass. 02108, U.S.A.
Printed in Great Britain by
Northumberland Press Limited, Gateshead
© I. A. Snook, 1972
No part of this book may be reproduced in
any form without permission from the
publisher, except for the quotation of brief
passages in criticism
ISBN 0 7100 7222 8
Set in 10pt Pilgrim on 12pt body

THE STUDENTS LIBRARY OF EDUCATION has been designed to meet the needs of students of Education at Colleges of Education and at University Institutes and Departments. It will also be valuable for practising teachers and educationists. The series takes full account of the latest developments in teacher-training and of new methods and approaches in education. Separate volumes will provide authoritative and up-to-date accounts of the topics within the major fields of sociology, philosophy and history of education, educational psychology, and method. Care has been taken that specialist topics are treated lucidly and usefully for the non-specialist reader. Altogether, the Students Library of Education will provide a comprehensive introduction and guide to anyone concerned with the study of education, and with educational theory and practice.

J. W. TIBBLE

In a liberal society such as ours the fear of indoctrination is widespread. Yet there is little clarity about what indoctrination is. Some think that moral and religious education *must* involve some element of indoctrination. Others think that indoctrination is inevitable with young children. And others even suppose that to tell a child something, as distinct from letting him find it out for himself, is to indoctrinate him. What, then, are the main features which distinguish indoctrination from other methods of passing on beliefs? And, if it is morally undesirable, what makes it so?

In this monograph Dr Snook judiciously sets out his own views in a way which takes account of current conceptions of indoctrination. He writes with a clarity and economy which should commend his work to those who are interested in the issues but unfamiliar with recent work in philosophy of education. For this monograph is to be regarded as complementary to Dr Snook's own *Concepts of Indoctrination: Philosophical Essays* in the International Library of Philosophy of Education in which he has collected this recent work together.

RICHARD PETERS

Contents

CONTENTS

Acknowledgments

The author acknowledges his debt to Professor R. S. Peters and Mr Philip Steedman for their valuable criticisms. They are, of course, in no way responsible for defects in the monograph. He wishes also to thank Miss Shirley Freeman and Mrs Gwen Standring who, in addition to their normal departmental duties, typed the manuscript with accuracy and unfailing good humour.

1
Introduction

'Indoctrination' belongs to a family of concepts which includes 'teaching', 'education', 'instruction', and 'learning'. It is, therefore, of concern to the educationist. It also has affinities with concepts such as 'bad', 'dishonest', 'unjust', and 'immoral'. For this reason it is of interest to the moral philosopher.

Since the concept is of some importance to both fields of study it is not surprising that both educationists and philosophers have shown an interest in it. The Progressivists in the United States paid a great deal of attention to this concept, and analytic philosophers have recently revived interest in it. It is clearly a topic which must find a home in the growing field of philosophy of education.

The method followed in this book is that of conceptual analysis. The writer believes that although there is some agreement as to the meaning of 'indoctrination' the agreement is mainly centred on its pejorative implications. Most would agree that to say to someone 'you are indoctrinating' is to criticize him. The reply 'yes, that is so' seems singularly inappropriate. A denial or at least an excuse seems to be required.

With words which are used with overtones of moral

criticism, disagreement can take place at any of three levels. Firstly, there can be argument about whether the term really does have pejorative implications. Secondly, there can be disagreement on the actual meaning of the term. Finally, there is room for dispute over whether in a particular case the conditions for the application of the term are fulfilled.

Take, for example, the word 'ambitious'. Two people might argue about this in the following ways:

1   One might hold that the term is pejorative, so that to say of a man that he is ambitious is automatically to censure him. The opponent might deny this and say that we can describe a person as ambitious without implying that he is worthy of blame. In this case, there may be agreement about the use of the term 'ambitious'. The disagreement is one of *values*.

2   They might instead differ over what sort of behaviour is to count as ambition. One might argue that a man who works hard, studies in his spare time, and keeps on friendly terms with his superiors is ambitious. The other might say that only rather special cases merit the description: a man must exemplify these traits to an unusual degree before 'ambitious' becomes an appropriate term to describe him. He must, for example, study more than others, go out of his way to cultivate the boss, and perform his duties in a manner out of all proportion to the recompense he receives. There is disagreement about the *concept*.

3   If agreement is reached as to the appropriate criteria for the use of the term, the two might still disagree over whether Charles is ambitious. The disagreement now is not conceptual but factual: does Charles in fact behave in a way which merits the term 'ambitious' being applied to

him? To find this out we do not study a concept. We have to study Charles. The disagreement is about *facts*.

The term 'indoctrination' can arouse similar dispute. People may differ over whether 'indoctrination' entails a criticism. They may argue about the meaning of the word. They may differ as to whether Mr Brown is indoctrinating.

This book is concerned with the second kind of disagreement. It deals with the concept of 'indoctrination'. Disputes about whether a particular teacher is indoctrinating have to be settled by investigation. But investigation cannot begin until there is some agreement about the concept. Just as we cannot identify an ambitious man without some understanding of what counts as ambitious behaviour, so we cannot discover whether a teacher is indoctrinating without a reasonable notion of what indoctrination is. Analysis is a first step towards identification.

The reader might agree that analysis is needed before investigation but argue that, even prior to this, the claim that indoctrination is morally wrong has to be proved. This critic might say that instead of analysing the concept the writer would be better employed on a work of moral philosophy aimed at showing why indoctrination is to be condemned. I have rejected this approach for three reasons:

1 It is notoriously difficult to present an ultimate justification for values. It is easier to secure agreement that murder is wrong than to show why it is. It is my conviction that once indoctrination is clearly understood, it will be obvious that it is reprehensible, although there will be disagreements as to why it is.

2 It cannot be shown that indoctrination is wrong if there is ambiguity about what it is. That there is ambiguity will be demonstrated throughout this book. Unlike

basic ethical disputes, conceptual ambiguities can be resolved or at least minimized by analysis.

3 Even if it is denied that 'indoctrination' is always pejorative, it cannot be denied that it often is. Once this is admitted it becomes necessary to distinguish the unfavourable sense of the term from the neutral (or favourable) sense. The search for the distinguishing criteria would involve the same kind of analysis as is attempted here.

For these reasons, I have assumed that indoctrination is always blameworthy and have concentrated on trying to discover its nature. If the reader believes that this restriction is unwarranted, he can wherever 'indoctrination' is used, substitute 'indoctrination*' where 'indoctrination*' means 'indoctrination in its pejorative sense'.

Some cases

It is first necessary to become aware that there is confusion in the use of the term 'indoctrination'. Let us look at some cases which might be called indoctrination and then sit in on a discussion in which some reasonably sophisticated people discuss these cases.

1 A Communist teacher in a Communist country teaches in such a way that the class is convinced that Communism is the only political system worthy of support.

2 A convinced Communist teaching in an English or American school tries hard to convert the class to Communism.

3 A teacher of literature knows that his interpretation of a literary work is disputed by many authorities but he makes no mention of these and presents his interpretation as the correct one.

4 As part of a research project, a student-teacher teaches what he knows is false (wrong dates, places, proofs etc.).

5 A parent tells a young child, 'Put away your toys: you must always be tidy.'

6 A teacher stresses rote learning for the tables, lists of Latin verbs, and major world capitals.

7 A parent unconsciously influences her children who adopt her standards, values, and attitudes.

8 A teacher of religion believes that certain doctrines are true and teaches them as if they are true.

Dialogue

Leader: You have looked at these cases. The question I want you to consider is this: which of these are cases of indoctrination?

Shirley: I think they all are.

Leader: Why?

Shirley: The teacher or parent in each case is not giving reasons. He's just influencing the children. He's not treating them as rational beings.

Michael: Well, you don't really know that, Shirley. I mean it isn't obvious from the cases that this is so. The Communist teacher might in fact be giving a good set of reasons for accepting Communism.

Shirley: But there isn't a good set of reasons for accepting Communism. Communism is an irrational system.

Michael: So you want to judge Communism? Aren't you just assuming that our Western values are right?

Shirley: I don't think so. After all I also said that the teacher of religion is indoctrinating and I am a Christian so I think I am being quite fair about this.

Anne: Let's take up that example of the teacher of religion. Suppose she did allow discussion and did give reasons for accepting the doctrines, what then?

Shirley: Then she wouldn't be indoctrinating, would she? The case is quite different.

Leader: But in reply to Michael, you said that a similar change in method by the Communist would not get *him* off the hook. Why the difference?

Shirley: Well, Christianity is basically rational, Communism isn't, that's all.

Anne: I think Shirley has got herself into a bind. She is caught between an objective standard—giving reasons—and her own subjective view about Communism. Surely, we cannot allow our own evaluation of a belief system to influence our idea of indoctrination. Otherwise it will be just a term with which to label what others do and will never apply to what we do.

Leader: What do you suggest, Anne?

Anne: Unlike Shirley, I don't think many of these cases are indoctrination at all. Things like literature, Latin, tables, tidiness aren't the sorts of things at all that we mean when we talk about indoctrination. We don't talk about indoctrinating Latin; we talk of indoctrinating Communism or something like that.

Michael: Yes, but what about the student involved in a research project (case 4)? The things that teacher is drumming in are much more like your Latin verbs than they are like Communism. Wouldn't you call what he is doing indoctrination?

Anne: No, he is just telling lies, that's all.

John: I can't accept that. Surely teaching what is false is indoctrination whatever else is. The teacher knows that the pupils are going to end up with false ideas.

Leader: You think that indoctrination is concerned somehow with what the teacher wants to do?

John: Yes I think so. An indoctrinator wants the pupil to
end up with false ideas.

Michael: Well, who is to decide what a false idea is?
Apart from the rare case I would think that indoctrinators believe that what they are teaching is true. They
are quite sincere.

John: Then they are not indoctrinating.

Anne: So a sincere belief is all that is required on the
part of the teacher?

John: Yes.

Anne: Then there is no objective criterion of indoctrination at all. No matter what he is teaching, so long as
he's sincere that's all right. It seems pretty odd to me.
You are entitled to teach children anything you think
is true?

John: When you put it like that, it doesn't seem quite
right. Perhaps, there is some relationship to what is generally accepted in society.

Leader: So perhaps the Communist in England is indoctrinating where the same person in Russia would not
be?

John: Yes, something like that, I think. Values are relative
after all.

Michael: But we are not talking about values. We are
talking about alleged facts: dogmas of Christianity,
scientific statements, history. Surely, facts are not relative. I mean, if it's true here it's true in China—surely?

Leader: Michael, you have been critical of what all the
others have proposed. What do you think about these
cases?

Michael: I don't think we can tell whether any of these

are cases of indoctrination. We would need to look at the end-product—the person being taught. An indoctrinated person, to my mind, is one who just can't think straight about some matters. He is one-eyed. He can't examine evidence or really consider another point of view. If any of the pupils in these cases end up like that they are indoctrinated. If not, then they're not.

Anne: We can only tell afterwards?

Michael: Yes.

Anne: How would we know whether their ultimate state was related to what was done to them by the teacher?

Michael: Just by common sense, I suppose.

Shirley: Anne is saying, I think, that people can be 'one-eyed' for a variety of causes—temperament, lack of experience or education—oh, hosts of things. Surely indoctrination is only one such cause.

John: Yes, that is dead right. We use 'indoctrination' to refer to a process. But it can be successful or unsuccessful. Michael, you imply that if it isn't successful, it isn't indoctrination.

Michael: If murder isn't successful, it isn't murder.

John: I suppose that's right up to a point. We don't *call* it murder but then we don't excuse it either. We hold the person responsible for trying and I guess we would do the same for indoctrination. That's why I think of indoctrination in terms of what the teacher wants to do, tries to do.

Anne: Well, what is it that an indoctrinator wants to do as against what any teacher wants to do?

John: The indoctrinator wants the pupils to hold on to the beliefs firmly.

Anne: Not any beliefs, surely—a teacher wants arith-

metical beliefs held firmly. We wouldn't want to call
her an indoctrinator.

John: False beliefs or beliefs that are not generally accepted in a society—the sort of qualification I mentioned
earlier.

Michael: It seems to me nonsense to suggest that teaching
religion in Russia is indoctrination when teaching it in
England is not. If anything, it should be round the other
way. It is precisely when certain ideas are widely held in
a culture that indoctrination is most likely to occur. It
would be difficult to indoctrinate Communism here but
easy to indoctrinate Christianity.

Leader: Well, let's see where we stand now concerning
these cases. Shirley believes that they are all cases of
indoctrination since the methods used are non-rational.
However, in the case of Communism she refuses to
allow that a rational presentation is possible. She is
forced then to adjudicate on which beliefs are rational
and this, as Anne pointed out, leaves the concept of
indoctrination open to individual interpretation, which
just won't do at all. Any comments, Shirley?

Shirley: I still think that indoctrination is related to
whether the teacher gives reasons or not. Perhaps I
should have said that if the Communist teacher gives
reasons he is not indoctrinating—though I feel somehow he is.

John: You feel this, I think, because you realize that you
can give reasons and still want to convince the pupils
that you are right. That's why I believe that the teacher's
aims are crucial.

Leader: But then, John, you link aims with content and
talk about false beliefs. This means that only case 4 is
clearly indoctrination, and this is a most rare case. One

9

or two of the others might be if in fact the political or religious beliefs are false or not generally accepted. Your view isn't really of much help to us in sorting out the cases since, once again, it's up to us to judge whether these beliefs are true or not.

John: Yes, it is a bit messy all right. But I can't seem to get away from the idea that what the teacher is trying to do is the decisive factor. But I do see the force of Anne's objection that whatever I put in after 'trying...' fails to distinguish indoctrination from ordinary teaching. Suppose I say 'trying to get the pupils to learn', this is near to a definition of 'teaching'. If I say 'trying to get the pupils to learn what is false' all the indoctrinators in the world will sit back contentedly and say, 'That counts us out: our beliefs are true.' I just don't know what to say now really.

Leader: Anne's view might help you out: didn't you say something about only some kinds of beliefs being subject to indoctrination, Anne?

Anne: Yes, I did, and since I last spoke I have been playing around with the word 'indoctrination'. It's related to 'doctrines' so perhaps we have it there: you can only indoctrinate doctrines.

Leader: So you would accept only the cases which deal with political and religious doctrines as valid cases of indoctrination?

Anne: That's my feeling at the moment.

Michael: It won't do.

Anne: Why not?

Michael: Couldn't a teacher discuss Communism without being accused of indoctrinating?

Anne: That's different from the case of the teacher who wants the child to believe in Communism.

John: Now you're on my side. The teacher's aims are important.

Michael: Around we go again! Well, look at it this way: some people are convinced Christians or Communists or whatever you like but are still fair and open-minded. I wouldn't call them indoctrinated. On the other hand some people are dogmatic about art, literature, sport. I'd call them indoctrinated although there are no doctrines involved.

John: I just don't think you can presume they are indoctrinated. They may just be narrow-minded by nature.

Leader: Looks as if we are now more confused than ever. Which is as it should be, you know. Spencer argued that men move from the unanimity of the ignorant, through the disagreement of the inquirer, to the unanimity of the wise, and he believed that the second stage is the parent of the third. We have moved into the second stage anyway and have begun to see that there is a problem. And that's a good beginning.

Discussion

The dialogue, inconclusive as it was, is suggestive of some notions both about conceptual analysis in general and the analysis of 'indoctrination' in particular.

CONCEPTUAL ANALYSIS

1 The attempt to clarify a concept is only possible among people of a certain sophistication. The man in the street can get by with only a vague or intuitive notion. He can use 'honest' fairly accurately without being very clear about its meaning. The lawyer and the policeman,

however, need to be much more clear. It is the contention of this book that students of education should have more clarity about 'indoctrination' than the layman.

2   There is no absolutely correct analysis. In a sense, each participant is entitled to his or her view of indoctrination. There is no one who can say with authority: 'You may not use the word in that way.' Words do not have meanings in the way that physical objects have weight. There are methods for establishing the weight of a stone; there are no similar ways of assessing the meaning of a word.

3   Nevertheless, it is not simply a matter of taste, about which no useful dispute is possible. Once the participants began to discuss the topic rationally they began to see that some of their views were untenable. They could not be sustained because either (a) they were internally inconsistent (e.g. Shirley's failure to distinguish between giving reasons for Christianity and giving reasons for Communism) or (b) they failed to make the distinctions which the participants wanted to make between indoctrination and other forms of teaching (e.g. John's problem with the aims of the teacher).

4   Hence there was some yielding of extreme positions. Shirley backed down on her distinction between Communism and Christianity. John became less sure of his criterion of aims and towards the end of the discussion Michael became a trifle less secure in his stress on consequences.

In the chapters to come a procedure similar to that followed by these people will be used. Various criteria of indoctrination will be suggested and I shall seek to show their inadequacy. I shall then argue for an analysis which, in my view, (a) takes care of the main cases that suggest themselves; (b) is internally consistent; and (c) enables us to make the distinctions which are important for the educationist.

The important thing is not that the reader agree with my conclusions but that he engage with me in the process of analysis. By so doing he will become clearer about 'indoctrination' even if he is unable to accept my conclusion.

THE CONCEPT OF INDOCTRINATION

All the participants had something reasonably plausible to say. Each suggested a criterion which seems to have something to do with indoctrination. None, for example, suggested that class-size, colour of the teacher's hair, or the state of the weather were relevant to the problem. Basically, they suggested four criteria: the method used by the teacher, the teacher's aims, the status of the beliefs imparted and the consequences on the mental life of the pupils. It seems plausible to argue that all of these are somehow related to indoctrination.

What needs to be distinguished, however, is what is *conceptually* related and what is only *factually* related. This distinction is important but not always easy to draw. An example may help a little. The concept of a 'bachelor' is one beloved of philosophers. Conceptually related to this term are the features (i) being unmarried, and (ii) being male. The term cannot be properly used without these criteria being satisfied. Suppose, however, that a survey showed that 90 per cent of bachelors are in fact self-centred and this becomes widely known. The term 'bachelor' now becomes associated with egocentrism so that when we think of a bachelor we think of a selfish person. The connection, however, is factual, not conceptual: one could still say without contradicting himself, 'He is a bachelor but is not self-centred.' One could not say without contradiction, 'He is a bachelor but is not a male.'

In analysing 'indoctrination' the problem becomes that of separating the features which are factually related from those which are conceptually related. Suppose, for example, we agree that an indoctrinator uses non-rational techniques. If this is conceptually related we will be unable to say with consistency: 'He indoctrinated but used a rational technique.' If, however, we do not find this absurd we shall probably have to conclude that the relationship is only factual: that by and large indoctrination does involve non-rational techniques but that this is a fact about the world, and is not entailed in the concept.

A word of caution is called for, though. No matter how hard we try, it is unlikely that we will get for 'indoctrination' a criterion or set of criteria as tight as is possible for 'bachelor'. An abstract concept like 'ambition', 'justice', or 'indoctrination' resists such analysis. Yet it is these concepts which are worth analysing; who wants to analyse 'bachelor', 'table', or 'tomato sandwich'? We take the trouble to analyse terms about which clarity is really important. It is my belief that 'indoctrination' is eminently worthy of our close and careful study for it has implications for the minds of men.

In the pages to come, this problem will be pursued. In chapter 2, the criteria already suggested by the participants will be critically examined. In chapter 3, the writer will present his analysis as it emerges from the discussion in chapter 2. In chapter 4, the analysis will be related to the teaching of morals, politics, and religion. The writer will use religion to exemplify how even in an area such as this, it may be possible to avoid indoctrination. Chapter 5 will relate indoctrination to other concepts: teaching, education, propaganda, conditioning, brainwashing.

2

Criteria of indoctrination

Preliminary considerations

As we attempt to clarify the concept of 'indoctrination', we must remember that concepts are related to the use of words. The way in which a word is used changes over the years and at any one time there are national, regional, and individual variations. The concept of indoctrination exemplifies these features of historical development and cultural variations. Gatchel (1959) has traced the evolution of the concept. He points out that the term originally meant the implanting of doctrines, 'doctrine' being synonymous with the noun 'teaching'. Because of the pre-eminence of the Roman Catholic Church in the middle ages, the term 'doctrine' came to mean Christian doctrine or the teaching of the Church. At the same time, education became very much a matter of handing on religious belief, and 'indoctrination' was used to designate the whole educational process. Gatchel argues that this conflation of the terms 'education' and 'indoctrination' can be viewed in either of two ways: (i) the term 'indoctrination' was broadened to include the whole process of education; or (ii) education became restricted to the implanting of church

doctrines and hence the term 'education' became synonymous with 'indoctrination'.

One thing is clear. There was no pejorative overtone to
'indoctrination' at this time. The development of democratic notions in politics and their extension to the field
of education brought about a split between the two concepts. 'Indoctrination' became associated with totalitarian
regimes and the coercive educational methods they were
supposed to use. 'Education' became restricted to the
humane and rational process of instruction which democratic states were presumed to practise.

Later on in this chapter we shall note how this naïve
distinction led to conceptual confusion and to bitter dispute on the practical level. It is hard to find a better
argument for conceptual clarity in education than in the
disputes which occurred in the United States during the
1930s. For the moment, however, it is sufficient to make
the point that in the United States, the debates surrounding indoctrination have centred on politics. This is a reflec-
tion of the historical development of the concept and the
particular concerns of American educators. In England,
the situation is different. The term 'indoctrination' has
tended to preserve its connection with the teaching of
Christian doctrine, at least in the minds of those who are
opposed to such teaching. The fact that religion has formed
an integral part of the school programme in England, but
not in the United States, helps to explain this national
difference. So pronounced is the variation in the focus of
interest and style of argument that there are two distinct
bodies of literature on the subject. The American corpus
is concerned with politics and it appeared in the 1930s and
1940s. The English corpus is largely 'analytic' in tone, deals
with the teaching of religion or morals, and is of recent

origin. It will be our task to attempt to synthesize these two groups of writings and to distil from them some commonality in the use of the term 'indoctrination'.

One of the hindrances to analysing 'indoctrination' is that there is a strong tendency to reserve it for the activities of those whose beliefs we dislike: what we ourselves do is almost never seen as indoctrination. Any adequate account of 'indoctrination' must be such that the term can be applied impartially to friend and foe alike. If this is not achieved, 'indoctrination' will remain solely a term of abuse, little better than a swear word. If 'indoctrination' is to function in educational theory, we must do better than this. When we say that someone is indoctrinating we do not just mean that we dislike what he is doing, although we do mean that we dislike what he is doing. We mean that there is something about what he is doing that we dislike. If we are objecting only to the content he is purveying the statement 'you are indoctrinating' means only 'I don't like *your* beliefs' and he can say the same to us. No further discussion is warranted and the term 'indoctrinate' becomes quite useless for appraising activities in an educational context.

We have already seen that analyses of 'indoctrination' typically centre on methods of teaching, the content of the lessons, the consequences of instruction, and the aims or intentions of the teacher. We will take each of these in turn and assess their adequacy in providing a criterion for using the term 'indoctrination'.

The method criterion

That indoctrination is a special method of teaching has support from history, from a common usage, and from some philosophical analyses of the concept of 'teaching'. We shall examine each of these in order to see the case for method at its full strength before proceeding to show its inadequacy.

In everyday life, people do say 'he is indoctrinating his pupils' and they seem to mean that something he is doing prompts this statement. Similarly, if an American says that the Communists indoctrinate their students there is the suggestion that they 'drum things in', indulge in brainwashing, or use harsh authoritarian methods.

It was this belief that encouraged the Progressivists in the United States to think of indoctrination as the method used by totalitarian regimes as distinct from the more humane methods favoured by democrats. When the Reconstructionist wing of the movement began to campaign for social reform through the schools, it became absolutely vital for them to insist on method as the criterion of indoctrination. For, like the Fascists or the Communists, they wanted to bring children to a new vision of society. It was no longer possible, they argued, for teachers to remain neutral on the pressing social issues of the day. They must exhibit 'defensible partiality' (Brameld, 1956, p. 201).

What distinguished them from others who used the school for social purposes was, they argued, that they encouraged discussion, stressed scientific method, and were utterly opposed to any distortion or suppression of evidence. Their critics quickly pointed out that they could not have it both ways. If the method was really so open, there was no reason to expect that the Reconstructionist view would prevail. If teachers were determined that it should prevail, then they could not escape the charge of indoctrination by reference to method. (For a succinct account of this controversy, see Bowers, 1969, pp. 116-22.) Nevertheless, despite these very real conceptual problems, educators in the United States have tended to equate indoctrination with a method of teaching. A recent writer has suggested that 'Dewey's type of outlook has so permeated American educational thinking that we automatically deal with this concept in terms of method only' (Moore, 1966, p. 398).

The analytic philosophers who have dealt with 'indoctrination' directly have all rejected the method criterion. However, some of those who have analysed the concept of 'teaching' have conveyed the impression that indoctrination is a particular method of bringing about belief. Many of them have written into the concept of 'teaching' a restriction of manner. Activities may look like teaching but because the restrictions are violated in some way they do not constitute teaching at all but something else, such as moralizing, preaching, or indoctrination. Scheffler (1960, p. 57), for example, argues that teaching requires us to submit our reasons to the student for his critical evaluation. Jane R. Martin suggests that if a teacher tries to prevent a pupil from acquiring any backing for his beliefs other than the say-so of an irrelevant authority, he is 'not teaching but is doing something else, for example, indoctrinating' (Martin, 1970, p. 102). In these as in other accounts of teaching, a procedural restriction is incorporated in the concept of 'teaching' and the way is open to exclude indoctrination from teaching on grounds of the method used.

Before attacking the method criterion directly, these three basic supports have to be undermined. The analytic argument, it seems to me, rests on a faulty analysis of 'teaching'. We may want to hold that for good teaching

20

or educative teaching certain procedures are unacceptable but it is just a mistake to say that the concept itself excludes them. In ordinary language we do speak of teaching a child to talk, teaching people what is false, and teaching without concern for understanding. The concept 'teaching', far from being a restrictive concept, is in fact the most general concept of the educational repertoire. 'Education' implies restrictions of value, 'instruction' suggests restrictions of method, 'training' entails restrictions of content. If indoctrination is to be analysed correctly it will not be by excluding it from the class of activities called teaching. Rather, clarity will be secured only by determining what sorts of teaching qualify as indoctrination.

The argument from ordinary usage can be disposed of by pointing out that terms which characterize human action are frequently ambiguous. They seem to refer to certain pieces of behaviour but frequently imply instead a judgment on the circumstances in which the behaviour is performed. 'Running' can be described in behavioural terms. 'Racing' cannot. Reference is required to the circumstances surrounding the runner. Yet we describe a person as racing as if we were referring solely to his behaviour. Therefore, the fact that people often speak as if indoctrination were a specific type of activity does not entail that it is. It may be, but there are other possibilities.

The Reconstructionists insisted that indoctrination is a method of teaching and their usage persists in American educational thought. There is, however, a plausible explanation for this. They were caught on the horns of a dilemma and emphasis on method enabled them to escape. They wanted teachers to take sides on a social issue the correct solution of which was a matter of dispute. They

21

were unable to distinguish their programme from indoctrination on grounds of content (a social philosophy) or on grounds of aims (allegiance to this philosophy). They were compelled, therefore, to draw the distinction on grounds of method. As we shall see, this is a favourite ploy of those accused of indoctrinating. That a method criterion is often useful in this way does not force us to say that it is the correct one.

I take it, then, that it is an open question whether indoctrination is a particular method of teaching, and we will go on to examine this claim.

If it is a particular method, then presumably it is a method which is marked by characteristics such as the following: (i) the teacher is authoritarian, allowing little discussion or questioning; (ii) the content is drilled or 'drummed in' in some way; (iii) there are threats of some sort which are held over the children; (iv) free discussion is not allowed. These rather vague descriptions are usually summed up in the expression 'a non-rational method'. For the remainder of this section, I shall use this shorthand expression without attempting to define it more exactly. My point is that no matter how it is defined it is an inadequate criterion.

Arguments against the method criterion

1 The expression 'using a certain method' is vague and ambiguous. If a classroom lesson is analysed it is found that many different activities occur. The teacher explains concepts and rules, defines terms, poses questions, keeps order, sets homework, clarifies instructions, writes on the blackboard, supervises assignments, marks projects, acts as discussion leader, and so on. What method is he using?

It is difficult to answer this question or even to make sense of it.

If instead of looking at a lesson, we look at a school day, a school week, or a school year, we find the position still more complicated. The teacher, in his efforts to promote learning, does many things which can be variously described. If a person is an indoctrinator when he uses 'non-rational' techniques, is one hour of drill in a week enough to provoke the charge? If so, all teachers are indoctrinators and the charge loses its punch. If a certain amount of the disfavoured method is allowable, what proportion is needed to make the teacher an indoctrinator? 20 per cent? 40 per cent? 70 per cent? The decision seems quite arbitrary. Of course when we reach the point of applying a concept to an individual we may have to resort to some arbitrary demarcation. We may, for example, not call an employee lazy or dishonest if he sits down for 10 minutes, but if he sits down for 30 minutes we may do so. It would be absurd to suggest that 'sitting down for 30 minutes' is part of the meaning of 'lazy'. Similarly, we may use some arbitrary criteria for applying the term 'indoctrination' to a teacher's work, but it would be quite odd to incorporate these criteria into the concept. What we are looking for, it will be remembered, is a criterion conceptually related to 'indoctrination'.

2   Methods and their acceptability cannot be adequately assessed apart from the content being taught. If the headmaster is told that the children in room 47 are reciting, he does not automatically stride down to censure their teacher. If he is interested at all, he asks what they are reciting. If he is told they are chanting 'E-N-O-U-G-H spells *enough*' he settles back to his desk content that all is well in room 47. If he finds that the

children are reciting 'The prime minister is a scoundrel' or 'Long live the revolution' he may begin to worry. Even here his worry could easily be allayed by his being told that the statement was part of a song for the school concert, or a portion of the crowd scene in a play.

The point is that apart from the content being taught, method does not normally come up for *moral* assessment. Of course some methods would: if the teacher were burning the soles of the children's feet we would be inclined to say 'Desist!' rather than ask whether he were teaching history or poetry. Apart from these cases, the methods used for teaching most subjects are assessed pedagogically rather than morally. Only in relation to certain types of content does the moral appraisal normally apply. It seems, then, that method is an inadequate criterion since we must ask not only 'how is he teaching?' but also 'what is he teaching?' If method is to function in identifying the concept of 'indoctrination' it will have to be taken in conjunction with content.

3 With very young children, rational methods are rarely possible. When parents are training their children to acceptable social or moral behaviour, they find that reasoning is of little value. As Aristotle pointed out, morality begins with habits; only on this foundation can the child's reason be engaged. If we accept that the use of 'non-rational techniques' is the mark of indoctrination, we are forced to say that the child's early training must be indoctrination. Of course, it is open to us to say that, provided of course that we are using 'indoctrination' in some neutral sense. You will recall, however, that in this book we are concerned with 'indoctrination' in its pejorative sense. It would be rather odd to say, 'In the early years, it is all right to use indefensible methods'. This in

24

effect is what we would be saying if we said, 'Indoctrination (pejorative sense) is allowable when dealing with a young child.' So, even if we are inclined to say that *in some sense* early moral training involves indoctrination, we still have to answer two questions: (i) how does this differ morally from indoctrination practised on older children? and (ii) are there not important moral differences in the way even young children are trained? The use of 'indoctrination' for every manner of habit formation glosses over the important distinctions we are attempting to make. This problem is endemic to making method the criterion.

4   The three arguments given above serve to indicate that method is not a *sufficient* condition for calling an activity indoctrination: a person can use a 'non-rational method' without being accused of indoctrinating. Perhaps 'non-rational method' is a *necessary* condition: a person could not be indoctrinating if he uses a 'rational method'. If this is correct, a teacher who uses a non-rational method may or may not be indoctrinating, but a person who uses a rational method is certainly not an indoctrinator. This version of the argument is used a great deal in attempts to deny the charge of indoctrination. A person accused of indoctrinating frequently says: 'Oh no. Look at what I do. I give reasons for everything I teach. I encourage discussion and questioning. I cannot be accused of indoctrinating.' We have already noticed this form of argument being used by the Reconstructionists and it is a common gambit.

That method is not even a necessary condition can be demonstrated quite easily. Indoctrination is concerned with the handing on of beliefs. These beliefs are typically regarded by the indoctrinator as of some importance. He

25

wants the pupils to accept these beliefs fully. Since a degree of understanding is required for holding any belief, a completely non-rational technique could scarcely succeed in getting the beliefs across at all. Furthermore, the indoctrinator wants the students to be able to justify their beliefs to themselves and to defend them against criticisms. There may be situations in which this is not necessary. In an isolated and homogeneous society it may happen that the beliefs are never questioned and justification is never called for. But the existence of such a situation is a contingent matter and in the modern world it rarely occurs. It is more common for students to face a pluralistic world with its hostile and articulate critics.

In this situation, the indoctrinator who did *not* attempt to give arguments, meet objections, answer questions, would be obviously inefficient. Research on teaching method aims at producing more efficient ways of achieving learning. If he is wise, the indoctrinator will avail himself of this knowledge as avidly as the educator, for he too is concerned with efficiency of learning. In so far as it is plausible to argue that reason-giving is vital for learning, the indoctrinator will use this technique also. It is no final defence to the charge of indoctrination to show that reasons have been given. Indoctrination may involve 'non-rational methods' but it need not. Any connection is empirical not conceptual.

5 The final argument is not a conceptual argument and is perhaps not really an argument at all. The case against using method as the criterion must rest on the four arguments so far brought forward. However, once the force of these has been grasped it is interesting to note that the method criterion is used mainly by those who are frequently accused of indoctrinating. As we have seen, the

Reconstructionists used it in their rebuttal. A Roman Catholic text in philosophy of education explains that indoctrination occurs when conclusions are taught without the reasons being given (Dupuis and Nordberg, 1964, p. 69). As I have already argued, such a practice is best described as incompetent teaching. A teacher who instructed by giving conclusions but not the reasons for them should face a charge of inefficiency. It would not matter whether he was educating or indoctrinating: he would on the face of it be doing it badly.

'Non-rational method' is a totally unacceptable criterion of indoctrination. Its extreme vagueness renders it virtually unintelligible. It cannot function apart from the content taught. It fails to distinguish acceptable and unacceptable techniques with young children, and it makes no allowance for the efficient, cunning, or well-trained indoctrinator. That it is the stand-by of those most often accused of indoctrinating adds to our suspicion that it is not a good distinguishing factor.

The content criterion: doctrines

It can be said with reasonable accuracy that, whereas American writers stress method, philosophers of education in Great Britain typically argue that it is the content taught which determines whether indoctrination is taking place. They argue that 'indoctrination' is conceptually linked to 'doctrines'. Only doctrines can be indoctrinated. Peters, for example, argues that 'whatever else "indoctrination" may mean it obviously has something to do with doctrines, which are a species of beliefs' (Peters, 1966, p. 41). Passmore asserts that in cases of indoctrination 'the pupil is drilled ... in doctrines and in stock replies to

27

stock objections to doctrine' (Passmore, 1967, p. 194). Flew states bluntly, 'No doctrines, no indoctrination' (Flew, 1967, p. 283).

This position has initial plausibility. Etymologically the two words are connected: in-*doctrin*-ation, the passing on of doctrines. Also, we do in fact use the term 'indoctrination' primarily in reference to religious, political, and social beliefs—the sorts of things which are frequently described as doctrines.

Despite the widespread acceptance of this criterion and its initial plausibility, I want to argue against making doctrines an essential feature of the concept. In order to sustain my case, three things have to be done: (i) we must show that there are cases which we would call indoctrination, although no doctrines are involved; (ii) we must explain the initial plausibility of the doctrine criterion; and (iii) we must indicate that this criterion, instead of illuminating the concept, leads to greater confusion.

Arguments against the content criterion

1   Etymologically, the two terms are connected. Their origin is the Latin language in which *docere* meant 'to teach', and *doctrina* meant whatever was taught. 'Indoctrination' was equivalent to 'teaching'; 'doctrines' stood for what was taught. 'Indoctrination', then, could be adequately described as 'the imparting of doctrines'. As we have seen, however, both terms have evolved. 'Doctrines' became restricted to the teachings of the Church, and 'indoctrination' broadened to include the whole of education. Etymology is of little help here, for two reasons. One of these has already been pointed out by other critics of the content criterion. The other has escaped their notice.

28

White (1967, p. 183) has drawn attention to the fact that one meaning of 'doctrine' is 'anything taught'. On this reading, the criterion becomes empty: 'indoctrination' = 'teaching' and there is no point in the arguments about the evil of indoctrination. It seems to me that the authors of an article criticizing White's argument missed the point of it (Gregory and Woods, 1970, pp. 95-100). They point out that *in ordinary usage* 'doctrine' does have a limited connotation: we do not speak of arithmetical facts as doctrines. Of course they are right but the ordinary language argument is a different argument from the etymological one. It is true that a dictionary tells us little about ordinary usage, as Gregory and Woods point out. But a dictionary can tell us a good deal about etymology.

White's original article as he himself says (White, 1970, p. 107) was a reply to Flew (1966). In his article Flew made an etymological point: 'The reiteration of the root word *doctrine* may suggest, beneficially, the notion of a limitation on the possible content of indoctrination' (Flew, 1966, p. 284). The point that White makes is, then, perfectly valid. What he wants to say is that even if we accept etymology as a relevant factor in the analysis, we do not have to concede that 'indoctrination' is necessarily connected with doctrines in the narrower sense. For the term 'doctrine' is systematically ambiguous. As an attack on the etymological argument (but not on the ordinary usage argument), White's point must be taken.

Against those who argue on etymological grounds, there is yet another argument. We have seen that doctrines were originally whatever was taught: geography, mathematics, history could be called doctrines. Subsequently, doctrines became restricted to the teachings of the Church. It follows that 'doctrines' could refer either to anything at all or simply to religious beliefs. But those who want to establish a conceptual link between 'indoctrination' and 'doctrines' subscribe to *neither* of these views. They want to limit the possible content of indoctrination but they do not want to limit it to religious matters. They want to extend it to other 'doctrinal' matters such as politics, history, and morals. In a sense there is no etymological warrant for their views at all.

Of course, they could argue that there has been a further development and 'doctrines' now refers to a wider range of matters than religious beliefs. The argument now begins to move towards 'ordinary usage', which will be discussed later. For the time being it is sufficient to point out that (i) it is not altogether obvious that we do speak of political doctrines, historical doctrines, and social doctrines, and (ii) that even if we do it may be because of some feature they share with religious beliefs, and it is *this feature*, not 'doctrine' itself, which is conceptually related to 'indoctrination'. Suppose, for example, that there occurred a development something like this. People noticed that religion was the sort of subject that encouraged a biased presentation of fact. Following the 'doctrine' lead, they termed such a biased method 'indoctrination'. Later, they noticed that other areas were similarly prone to biased teaching (history, politics, morals) and so they used 'indoctrination' to refer to that and, to indicate their dislike for what was imparted, called these beliefs doctrines also. On this reading, 'doctrines' and 'indoctrination' would be related but only contingently so. 'Indoctrination' would be conceptually connected to something else, such as the method of teaching.

I have already argued against the method criterion. The point of reintroducing it here is to support the argument that etymology and ordinary usage do not force us to accept that 'doctrines' and 'indoctrination' are conceptually connected.

2 A second objection against this link is that even in what seem to be the paradigm cases of doctrines (political and religious beliefs), there must be a non-indoctrinating way of dealing with them. Assuming for the moment that 'doctrines' can be adequately defined, would we not want to say that there are legitimate ways of handling political, moral, and religious issues within an educational context? If it is indoctrination to deal with such matters, the political scientist and the philosopher of religion are indoctrinators because their subject matter is, in part, political theories and religious statements respectively. Since I do not believe that anyone would really want to hold this, there must be something wrong in the suggestion that doctrinal content is a sufficient condition. It may, of course, be a necessary one.

In our analysis, there must remain the possibility of religious, moral, and political *education*. Whatever these will consist in, we will want to avoid both a mere outlining of various positions and indoctrination. The recounting of what others believe could not constitute an education in the religious, moral, or political modes of thought. On the other hand, indoctrination in a particular view is to be avoided on ethical grounds. If these are the alternatives, we cannot be surprised if the community and the teaching profession choose indoctrination. The task of the educationist is to provide a viable third alternative. The danger inherent in making a close link between 'doctrines' and 'indoctrination' is that the way is closed off for the development of justifiable courses of study in religion, politics, and morals.

3   So far, I have presented a counter-argument against the etymological point and an argument based on the insufficiency of the content criterion. The principal argument, however, rests on the extreme vagueness of the concept of 'doctrines'. If the claim 'indoctrination is concerned with doctrines' is to be taken seriously we need to know what is connoted by the term 'doctrines'. Otherwise we have not been told anything. Strangely, most of those who have argued for doctrines as the criterion have not attempted any analysis of the term 'doctrine' which remains as vague as the 'indoctrination' it is meant to illuminate.

Attempts to define 'doctrines'

In two recent accounts of indoctrination attempts have been made to clarify the notion of a doctrine (Gregory and Woods, 1970; Gribble, 1969). These will be examined to see whether they provide criteria for distinguishing doctrines in a way which will assist us in our task of producing an analysis of 'indoctrination'.

1   Gregory and Woods argue that the salient characteristic of doctrines is that they are not known to be true or false. This, they suggest, distinguishes doctrines from manifest facts and from untruths. Assuming that it does this, we need to ask whether in general it distinguishes doctrinal matters from non-doctrinal ones. It is clear that it does not. Precise statements about the present population of a country are not known to be true or false, yet who would call such statements doctrines? The authors themselves cite an example which weakens their own case. They speak of the 'popular doctrine' that there is 'apathy among the voters' (p. 87). If opinions about the attitudes of

the citizens are doctrines, how far ahead are we in our discussion of either doctrines or indoctrination? If the statement 'indoctrination has to do with doctrines' simply means, 'indoctrination has to do with statements not known to be true or false' why don't we just say that instead of getting bogged down in 'doctrines'?

2 Perhaps the authors meant something more rigorous than they seemed to say. They may have had in mind some application of the verification principle. A doctrine would then become a statement which cannot *in principle* be shown to be either true or false. Facts about population may not in fact be known, but they could be known given sufficient interest and sophistication of methods and instruments. A statement such as 'democracy is fully in accord with human nature' is not, even in principle, susceptible to investigation. We would not know what it meant to verify (or falsify) this statement and so it is a doctrine.

Hopeful as this strategy may seem, it too is defective in separating doctrines from non-doctrines. For if by 'doctrine' we refer to individual propositions of a religious or political nature, many of these *are* verifiable in principle. That Christ rose from the dead, for example, is knowable in principle. If there is a difference between such a claim and more recognized claims ('Caesar crossed the Rubicon'), it does not rest on the possibility of verification.

If, however, the argument is that 'doctrine' does not refer to individual claims but to the whole corpus in which these claims occur ('Marxist doctrine', 'Roman Catholic doctrine') we again face a problem. On this account, science itself becomes a doctrine. For a science is a network of models, theories, and data, all interdependent. It is not possible to verify the whole corpus: indeed models are not really verifiable at all. If the strict principle of verification is applied to a science, it too becomes a doctrine.

Gregory and Woods (1970, pp. 87-8) seem to anticipate such a criticism and they try to guard against it by saying that a scientific statement is part of a complex theoretical system which is designed to explain certain phenomena. The difficulty with this is that a proponent of a religious, philosophical, or political system could make the same claim for the statements he makes. A Marxist, for example, could argue that his system is one which explains certain obvious facts (phenomena) about workers, industrialization, wars, and revolutions. Again, the distinction between science and 'doctrine' fades.

Similar objections apply to Gribble's attempts to define 'doctrines' (Gribble, 1969, p. 32). A doctrine, he argues, is a set of beliefs which rest on assumptions which are either false, or which cannot publicly be shown to be true. Against this it must be said that the fundamentals of a science cannot be shown to be true, unless we accept the pragmatic notion that theories which produce results are true. Science may be said to be pragmatic in this sense and it is no discredit to it. But if this line is pursued the same might be said of religious and political doctrine. If human consolation is desirable, religion 'works'; if the improvement of social conditions is a good thing, Communism 'works'. That is to say, if Gribble's criterion 'shown to be true' is interpreted strictly *neither* science *nor* religion qualifies. If it is interpreted pragmatically *both* science *and* religion qualify. In either case we are unable to distinguish doctrines from non-doctrines.

3 Gregory and Woods make a second attempt at distinguishing doctrines from non-doctrines. A doctrine, they say, is a statement not arrived at by scientific method.

This also fails as a distinguishing factor. The basic assumptions and postulates of an empirical science qualify as doctrines and many religious statements do not. A theologian, for example, could justly claim that what he does is as fully 'scientific' as what is done by an historian or literary critic.

Of course, there is an ambiguity about the honorific term 'scientific'. Gregory and Woods dismiss religion as scientific because it does not consist in 'the setting up of hypotheses and ... the subsequent attempt to confirm or disconfirm them experimentally'. Of course, the work of theologians is not scientific in this sense. But neither is that of geologists and historians. They claim to be scientific but this does not always involve experimental work. If one interprets 'scientific' in this strict sense, large areas of the humanities, social sciences, and some natural sciences are excluded and presumably become doctrines. To every historian it is possible to say 'you are indoctrinating'. 'Why?' 'Because you are imparting statements not arrived at by scientific (i.e. experimental) method.'

If, on the other hand, we use 'scientific' to refer to the careful and impartial consideration of data of any sort, the theologian or philosopher can claim that this is the way he proceeds.

Ah, says Gribble (1969, p. 34), but his conclusions are not *publicly* testable, and this is what distinguishes the work of geologists from the activities of theologians. Geologists succeed in convincing other scientists; theologians remain in warring camps. In the following chapter I shall argue that there is much merit in this distinction. What I deny, however, is that it is useful in distinguishing doctrines. As Gribble points out, economists, literary critics, historians, and social scientists face similar problems. Hence in these fields there exist various 'schools' with their own theories, adherents, and body of 'evidence'.

I do not want to deny that for an understanding of indoctrination it is important to make distinctions on the basis of the methods for gaining information and the degree of acceptance of the conclusions. It does seem, however, an unprofitable strategy to insist that indoctrination is concerned with doctrines and then to write into one's analysis of 'doctrines' the distinctions one wants to make between the procedures of the various content areas. There are, I think, more navigable rivers to the port.

4 So far, we have criticized the doctrine criterion because it is vague, and, however analysed, does not provide a sufficient condition. My final objection goes beyond this to argue that regardless of the way 'doctrines' are defined, they are not a necessary condition for indoctrination. The deliberate teaching of what is false must be subsumed under 'indoctrination'. I agree with White (1967) that if a teacher deliberately set out to teach his pupils that Melbourne is the capital of Australia, he would be indoctrinating even though no doctrines or ideologies were involved.

Gribble (1969, p. 32) argues against this on the grounds that although we *might* call this indoctrination we normally would just call it incompetent teaching, or 'telling lies' or something of that sort. Gribble suggests that philosophers get led into absurdities when they look for tight logical connections and search for what is conceivable rather than what we would in fact tend to say. This argument, too, is a forceful one. We cannot expect to get a perfectly tight set of criteria for a term such as 'indoctrination'. Nevertheless, I would argue that in the interests of clarity it is better to proceed as if we could. We should not be too ready to say: this is the criterion; cases which fall outside it are 'peripheral', or 'odd'. We may ultimately have to say something like this but we ought not to concede the field too easily. The search for a more inclusive criterion is the life-blood of analysis.

What really bothers us about the case of the teacher imparting inaccurate geographical information is that we cannot understand why he would want to do it. His action is not really intelligible without some reference to his motives. At this point, something like an ideology ('doctrine') is an obvious candidate. If the false information can be related to a political or religious creed, the action begins to make sense. If the Marxist philosophy requires a particular biological theory, the teaching of the latter by a Communist makes sense. If a Roman Catholic principle accords better with one set of medical information than with another, we understand why the Catholic stresses one rather than the other.

My contention is that doctrines enter into indoctrination as explanations. They explain many cases of indoctrination by furnishing the motive. That is why we do associate the term with ideologies. Those who are in favour of some system of doctrine are those who are most likely to indoctrinate. The connection which has seemed to some to be conceptual is instead motivational.

My conclusion then is that 'indoctrination' is not restricted to the teaching of doctrines, however these are defined. In practice, however, indoctrination is frequently associated with ideologies because these provide one of the most cogent motives for indoctrinating. Since other motives can be found, the presence of a 'doctrine' is not a necessary condition for indoctrination. Since there are

37

non-indoctrinating ways of handling doctrines, they are not a sufficient condition either.

Consequences as the criterion

In daily life we sometimes say disparagingly that a certain person is indoctrinated. We mean that in some area of human thought or activity, his mind is closed, his beliefs are not open to rational scrutiny. In this area at least, evidence, argument, and logic make no impression on him. He listens courteously perhaps while we present our case but when he speaks again, the impression we get is that what we have said has made no impression. If he argues at all, he views arguments not as rapiers for parry and thrust but as clubs with which to beat us into insensibility. We learn in time that there is no use talking to old so-and-so about politics (or religion or youth or gardening, as the case may be) and we leave him alone to his myths and prejudices.

It is very likely that the existence of people like this has led us to an awareness of the issue of indoctrination. That is to say, it may be a psychological fact that if there were no people like this we would not have the concept of indoctrination at all. It is, therefore, not surprising that some have attempted to equate the qualities shown by indoctrinated people with the concept itself. Green argues that indoctrination is distinguished from education in terms of the end-product: the indoctrinated person does not hold his beliefs 'evidentially'. He cannot 'give any adequate reasons for them, any clear account of them, or offer any sound evidence in their support' (Green, 1964-5, p. 299).

There is a good deal of validity in the suggestion that

the indoctrinated person does not hold his beliefs 'evidentially'. Later chapters will show the crucial position of evidence in the analysis of 'indoctrination'. But in his attempt to round out his notion of 'evidentially' held beliefs, Green leads us into further obscurity. For, (i) if he means that an indoctrinated person can say nothing in support of his beliefs, it is difficult to know to what extent they can be called beliefs. If, for example, I assert that there is life on Mars but refuse to give any justification at all for saying this, can I be said to believe that there is life on Mars? (ii) If he means that the person cannot say very much in support of his beliefs, I would be inclined to put this down to the inadequacy of his indoctrination. As I have argued before, there is no necessary connection between indoctrination and incompetent teaching. I would argue that the inability to give an account of one's beliefs, to offer some justification for them is as much the mark of defective teaching as it is of indoctrination. A truly indoctrinated person thrives on arguments for, as Passmore (1967, p. 194) points out, the drill in stock objections is often an important feature of the process of indoctrination. (iii) If Green wants to insist rather on his adjectives, '*adequate* reasons', '*clear* account', '*sound* evidence', the distinction between an indoctrinated person and anyone else is blurred. For in the uncertain areas of human discourse, these themselves are matters of dispute. We may think his reasons inadequate, his account unclear, his evidence unsound. He will make similar judgments about us. Who, then, is indoctrinated?

Arguments against consequences as the criterion

My critique so far has been directed against the actual

criteria Green suggests. I want now to go further and argue that whatever criteria we set up as distinguishing an 'indoctrinated' person, they will never be sufficient for asserting that indoctrination has taken place. Let us say that it is agreed empirically that indoctrinated people display a set of criteria which we call X. (This will probably subsume such traits as defensiveness when criticized, persistence with an argument even after it has been shown to be invalid, reliance on arguments from authority, refusal to admit mistakes etc., etc.)

1   The existence of criteria X will be explicable in many ways—low intelligence, temperament, home background, psychological problems, drugs, and so on. Indoctrination is only one possible explanation. If, for example, we have reason to believe that the person is like he is because of a motor accident, we do not call him indoctrinated. This means that we have to make clear what we mean by indoctrination as distinct from collisions, and the process of analysis has to begin again.

2   The reason for this is that 'indoctrination' is both a task and an achievement term. Peters (1966, p. 26) has argued that 'education' is also a task-achievement term : we speak of 'education' as a process (task) and we speak of an 'educated' man (achievement). There is, however, an important difference between the two words. In the case of 'education' the achievement sense is of prime importance and the task sense derivative. (In J. L. Austin's phrasing, the achievement sense 'wears the pants'.) 'Indoctrination', however, refers primarily to a process or activity and only secondarily to the successful achievement : the task sense 'wears the pants'. That is to say we would call a person educated if he displayed the signs of an educated man, whatever these may be. We would not

call a man indoctrinated unless we had reason to believe that he had been subjected to some process which we call indoctrination.

3 Since 'indoctrination' refers to some process, it follows that we can fail to indoctrinate. A person subjected to indoctrination may not succumb and so not display any of criteria X. Yet we would not say that his instructor had not been indoctrinating after all any more than we would withdraw the charge of stealing simply because the 'jewels' were fakes. Indoctrination can occur without anyone being indoctrinated. Consequences are neither a necessary nor a sufficient condition of indoctrination.

Intention as the criterion

One of the first writers to stress the intention criterion was William Heard Kilpatrick, a disciple of John Dewey and one of the leading Progressivists in the United States during the first half of this century. Although he allows for the possibility of unintentional indoctrination, Kilpatrick argues that in so far as indoctrination is an evil, intentions are the key criterion. In discussing the moral training of the young child, he argues that a parent cannot be accused of indoctrinating if she (i) intends to give reasons when it becomes possible to do so, and (ii) uses no methods which would inhibit free inquiry later (Kilpatrick, 1940, pp. 172-4; 1951, pp. 123-4). Kilpatrick's solution to the problem of moral training is an interesting one. On the one hand he stresses intention; on the other, he makes it clear that intentions are not mysterious and inaccessible qualities of a mind: they find expression in behaviour.

R. M. Hare (1964, pp. 50-4) has argued a similar view

with reference to moral training. He points out that two parents may do the same things (identical *method*) to their children to induce a certain moral attitude (identical *content*) and yet one may be indoctrinating, the other may not. For one is intending that this be the abiding attitude of the child, while the other intends that the child come to evaluate moral positions for himself. Hare goes on to make the point that the aim will have a bearing on content and method. But the aim is the primary thing: the others derive from it.

White (1967) also argues that indoctrination is distinguished from education by the intentions of the teacher. A teacher is an indoctrinator, argues White, if his intention is that the child should believe P in such a way that nothing will shake that belief.

Preliminary objections to intentions

This intention criterion can be attacked in a number of ways:

1 The claim might be made that the appropriateness of a particular intention will depend on the views of the parent or teacher on the nature of the subject matter in question. Hare and Kilpatrick, for example, would condemn the parent who taught the child that moral values are firm and objective. But what if moral values *are* firm and objective? What if the parent really believes that they are, even if they are not? Certainly he will not have as his aim that the child grow up free to reject them. Why should he, since he does not accept that they are the sorts of things one *is* free to reject? How can a teacher with this intention be called an indoctrinator? In his eyes, his intention is perfectly appropriate (Crittenden, 1968).

2 A second objection is that if the teacher has himself been indoctrinated, his intention will be the same as that of any good educator. He will sincerely claim that he wants his pupils to think for themselves, to evaluate what he says, and to come to their own conclusions. Since he himself believes that his position is completely rational, he will have no fear of arguments and discussion. He will feel as secure as the physics teacher that reason, evidence, and logic are on his side. His intention will not be in any way illiberal as described by Hare, Kilpatrick, and White. In fact it will be indistinguishable from the intention of any good teacher or parent: to hand on the truth in a reasonable manner.

3 It has also been argued that 'intention' is far too mysterious to function as the basis for determining indoctrination. Intentions are private, inaccessible entities. We can never determine whether a person is indoctrinating or not, unless we ask him. He has only to deny an indoctrinatory intention and the charge must lapse (Eckstein, 1969, p. 339).

It is my contention that in the notion of intention we come to the essential characteristic of indoctrination. I shall elaborate on this position in the next chapter. Suffice for the moment to sketch out the form of the strategy that will be needed to counteract these cogent arguments just presented against the intention criterion. I make no attempt to rebut them at this point. I want merely to convey some idea of the form the counter-arguments must take. In the next chapter I shall develop more fully these counter-arguments in the course of my discussion of intentions.

The first point to bear in mind is that in this book we are primarily concerned with a conceptual analysis of 'indoctrination'. We are looking for a criterion which is related to 'indoctrination' conceptually. Against this, pragmatic arguments are of no avail: difficulties of *applying* the criterion do not indicate that the criterion is faulty. An example may help. 'Stealing' involves the intention to keep what is taken. This is a conceptual point. That it is often difficult to determine whether someone did steal is a problem for policemen, lawyers, and judges. It is not a matter of concern to philosophers.

It is, nevertheless, necessary to make quite clear what we mean by 'having an intention'. Otherwise the intention criterion will be as vacuous as the content criterion was shown to be. In talking about 'intentions' we shall have to avoid any suggestion that they are utterly mysterious 'entities' about which nothing significant can be said, except by the person who has them.

Provision has to be made, therefore, for intentions which the agent might not admit to. Despite an initial strangeness, there is nothing essentially unusual about this. If a man is kicking a window, we can conclude that he intends to break it. That he disavows this intention does not alter the fact, unless he is completely unfamiliar with the nature of glass. That is to say, there are objective conditions which help to identify intentions. The admission of an intention is not always required, although it sometimes is, when the objective description of an act is not clear—e.g. 'Are you chopping that tree down or are you merely ringbarking it?'

Conclusion

In this chapter we have examined four possible criteria of 'indoctrination': method, content, consequences, and intention. I have argued that method, content, and consequences fail as criteria for 'indoctrination'. I have suggested that 'intention' will provide an adequate criterion but have pointed out that 'intention' itself needs careful analysis and that certain crucial objections have to be met.

In the next chapter I shall present and argue for a formulation of the intention criterion, attempt to meet the objections, and apply the criterion to some cases where the issue of indoctrination is liable to be raised.

3

Indoctrination and intentions

According to White (1967), indoctrination requires an intention of a certain sort, namely the intention that the child believes what is taught in such a way that nothing will shake his belief. I want to argue that this is close to being a correct analysis of 'indoctrination' but that, as stated and discussed by White, the criterion is still inadequate.

1   The intention to inculcate unshakeable beliefs may by a necessary condition but it is certainly not sufficient. Teachers of mathematics, chemistry, and Latin have to teach many things which they do not expect to be questioned, much less rejected. White's account does not cover our unwillingness to call those teachers indoctrinators.

2   His main example deals with a false proposition ('Melbourne is the capital of Australia'). He then has to carry on the argument in terms of a series of falsehoods. Since the point of the intention criterion is to shift attention from content, it is unfortunate that his examples suggest that what is true cannot be indoctrinated. His examples also deal with what the agent himself knows to be false or doubtful. He makes no allowance for the application of 'indoctrination' to the teaching of what is true and certain nor to the teaching of what is false or doubtful

when the agent does not know that it is false or doubtful.

These two criticisms are partially in opposition. On one hand, I criticize White because he seems to have 'indoctrination' cover the teaching of what is true and certain (mathematics, Latin, chemistry) and on the other, because he suggests that it does not. I seem to say that the analysis is both too strict and too lax. In the tension between these two positions the main problem of indoctrination lies. What has to be allowed for is (i) that it is *conceptually* possible to indoctrinate what is true and well established, and (ii) that *in fact*, most of the time, we do not want to apply the term 'indoctrination' in these cases. An adequate analysis must be able to account for both these facts.

I suggest that the following provides a necessary and sufficient condition of indoctrination: *A person indoctrinates P (a proposition or set of propositions) if he teaches with the intention that the pupil or pupils believe P regardless of the evidence.*

The remainder of this chapter will be devoted to explicating the various sections of this 'definition' and to showing how it can account for the various facets we have so far considered.

Indoctrination and teaching

In an earlier section I argued that to separate 'teaching' and 'indoctrination' is mistaken conceptually and dangerous in practice. Far from it being the case that 'teaching' excludes 'indoctrination', there is a *necessary* or *conceptual* relationship between them.

There is an ambiguity about 'teaching' which is important in the analysis of indoctrination. A small child may teach his mother, or a student teach his professor. Yet we would not say that the child indoctrinated his mother or the student his professor, regardless of the nature of the belief or the method used. Similarly, we can say that I taught the class a particular theorem on Tuesday afternoon; 'indoctrination' seems to resist close specification of time.

The reason for this is that 'teach' can refer to any intentional attempt to foster learning but that its other and more usual use is narrower. In the narrower sense, it suggests: (i) that the person teaching stands in a special relationship to the person taught, a relationship of some authority which gives the teacher a privileged role in the transaction; (ii) that there are teaching activities extended over a period of time. The noun 'teacher' captures this better than the verb. We do not call someone a teacher simply because on an occasion he 'teaches' someone something.

'Indoctrination' is related to this narrower sense of teach. It implies (i) some degree of authority-control and (ii) performance extended over time. In the formula given above, 'teaches' should be understood in this way.

This connection with 'teaching' helps to solve certain problems which continually crop up in discussions of indoctrination. For example, it has been suggested that a person who engages in an argument with a friend on a contentious issue might be an indoctrinator. Gregory and Woods (1970, p. 103) tell us that the two authors split company on the question whether or not a devout Catholic who tries to convince another person of the truth of the Catholic religion must be an indoctrinator. They parted company on the question because one argued that this could be done rationally while the other said it could not. Surely they both missed the point. The answer must be 'no' because 'indoctrination' does not figure in *any* inter-play of ideas but only in teaching situations. Certainly if all attempts to persuade others on contentious issues constitute indoctrination, most of us are indoctrinators. In fact, however, there is a world of difference between arguing a case in the drawing room, the philosophy seminar, or the executive suite and arguing it before one's students.

We might even (though with some hesitation) go further and suggest that 'indoctrination' is restricted to what is done to children. Perhaps the notion of indoctrinating adults makes little sense unless (i) it is the continuation of a process begun in youth OR (ii) special psychological weapons are used, making 'brainwashing' an appropriate term (see the section on brainwashing, chapter 5).

Even more absurd are the scruples of Gregory and Woods that they themselves might be indoctrinating in their article on indoctrination (1970, p. 103). If one can indoctrinate by writing a paper directed to one's academic colleagues, then it seems evident that the concept has been stretched beyond recognition. Part of this distortion can be attributed to their stress on doctrines: if any reliance on doctrine constitutes indoctrination then there *are* problems with any presentation of controversial state-ments. This is one reason why the notion of doctrines cannot be central to the concept. The other source of confusion is the neglect of the intimate connection with teaching. There is a distinction to be drawn between what we are entitled to say to our colleagues and what we can legitimately say to those who are our students.

Teaching and intentions

The phrase 'with the intention' leads us to examine the concept of 'intention'. 'Intention' is a difficult term to analyse since it is used in many different contexts each of which has its own problems. It is used here in the context of moral evaluation: only if there is the intention to impart beliefs regardless of the evidence can we apply the term 'indoctrination'. This moral context helps us to specify more accurately the phrase 'with the intention'. In the context of moral responsibility, 'intention' can connote (i) what is desired, and (ii) what is foreseen as likely. Thus, I want to argue that a person is indoctrinating if (i) in his teaching he is actively desiring that the pupils believe what he is teaching regardless of the evidence, or (ii) he foresees that as a result of his teaching such an outcome is likely or inevitable. That is, there is a strong and a weak sense of 'intend' (and 'intention') and the concept of indoctrination includes both.

In everyday usage, 'intention' is often restricted to the strong sense. We commonly use 'intention' to refer only to what we want to do, not to the inevitable by products of what we do. If I am hammering nails, and disturbing the neighbours, it is legitimate to ask what I am doing. My answer ('fixing the fence') specifies my intention and you may then say 'he does not intend to disturb the neighbours'. However, if the consequences involve harm to someone, it then becomes appropriate to speak of intentionally causing the harm even if I do not in any way desire that harm. If I persist in firing a rifle in a populated area, the fact that I intend (strong sense) to shoot birds does not excuse me if I should kill or injure a human being. It can be said that since I foresaw that possibility, I intentionally brought it about. It has been my contention throughout this book that the results of indoctrination are a matter for moral concern, and to act with the realization that they will follow is to act intentionally and so render the agent liable to moral criticism.

Arguments against intentions as the criterion

A number of objections can be raised to this criterion of intention and my rendering of it.

1   It might be objected that there are cases which we would term indoctrination which this criterion does not cover. The following examples might be suggested:

a   A mediaeval teacher is teaching that the world is flat. He is not intending (strong sense) that the pupils hold false beliefs nor does he foresee this. And yet, they are being led to hold beliefs which evidence does not support: they are being indoctrinated. To this, the reply must surely be, how is 'indoctrination' relevant here? The matter is not disputed, the evidence that exists confirms what is being taught. Why call it indoctrination *in any sense*? To accuse the mediaeval teacher of indoctrinating when no evidence contrary to his beliefs was available would be rather like accusing a nineteenth-century doctor of malpractice because he did not prescribe penicillin. In short, my reply to this example is that it would be unreasonable to call it indoctrination and hence the criterion is unaffected.

b   A more difficult problem is raised by the case of a person working within a system in which certain ideas are generally accepted as beyond question, although in a wider connection they are subject to dispute. Examples would be a Communist teacher in a Communist country, a Catholic teacher in a Catholic school, a racist teacher in a racist community. It will be objected that these people can be called indoctrinators despite the fact that they can claim that they do not desire or foresee that their beliefs will be held 'regardless of the evidence', for they have no reason to think that there is anything wrong with the evidence. I want to leave for a later section the problems associated with the connection between evidence and consensus but the objection against 'intention' as a criterion has to be dealt with here.

The problem, in brief, is this. An observer outside the system calls it 'indoctrination' (and in a pejorative sense). Yet an indoctrinating intention does not seem to be present. The intention criterion is, therefore, faulty.

The following lines of defence are open:

i It could be said that in these cases a full-blown intention *is* present, i.e. the teachers in the system are devoted to the cause and their main intention is that the beliefs be held. The evidence they give is secondary to the main purpose—the handing on of certain beliefs. So, they do in fact intend that the pupils believe P regardless of the evidence, although they are unaware of any evidence to the contrary.

ii The observer's charge of indoctrination can be viewed as an ascription of responsibility. Standing outside the system and aware of the insufficiency of the evidence, he judges that the inevitable result of the teaching will be that the pupils will hold beliefs for which the evidence is dubious. Consequently, he accuses the teacher of indoctrinating. It is rather like an observer who describes someone as a thief. The accused can then attempt to rebut the charge by reference to the facts ('these things are mine'), or to his state of mind ('I did not know they belonged to someone'). Similarly, the person accused of indoctrination can argue that because of his lack of knowledge, he could not be said to be acting intentionally. If the charge is valid, he then becomes aware of what he is doing and, if he continues, the charge of indoctrination is applicable in the full sense. He now foresees the results and 'intention' becomes appropriate.

At this point, my critic might argue that in 'solving' his initial problems two further ones have opened up.

2 'Come on now,' he might say, 'you went to great lengths to show the inadequacy of content, method, and consequences. You insisted that intentions could save the day. Now you write content and method into *your* notion of intention. How is your analysis in any way superior to any other?'

It is true that my notion of intention is grounded on what and how the teacher teaches. I would deny, however, that it is just another way of talking about content, method, or consequences. It has the advantage over these in that it can subsume any one of these singly or two or more of them conjointly. For example, if a teacher sets out to win a class for Christianity or 'democracy', he is indoctrinating because of his intention (strong sense) even if his method is totally 'rational'. If a teacher twists the evidence for his own purposes, he is indoctrinating, even if the content is quite undisputed. His intention (strong sense) is indoctrinatory although the content might seem to be excluded from that label. If a person in good faith teaches in such a way that the students are led to hold strong views on disputed issues, the charge is again appropriate because of the consequences which are intended (weak sense). That is to say, the intention is detected in content, method, or consequences but is not equivalent to any particular one, or any particular combination.

3 Another critic could argue that the intention criterion is totally useless. 'Surely,' he might say, 'the best judge of someone's intention is the agent himself. But you have suggested or implied that in some cases the agent may not even know he has the intention.'

I would agree that in normal circumstances the agent is the best judge of his intentions. However, this is not so where moral criticism is involved. 'I gave my excuse,' says the school boy. 'You lied,' says the teacher. 'I am resting,' says the employee. 'You are wasting time,' says her boss. 'I'm having a fling,' says the gay husband. 'You are being unfaithful,' says his frank friend. Each gives a description of sorts, the observer merely adding a moral criticism. Similarly with indoctrination. A person *might* say 'I am indoctrinating' but normally he would not. Indoctrination is intentional but the intention need not be one to indoctrinate in the sense that he would answer 'indoctrinating' when asked what he was doing. He would normally state his intention as one to teach.

This brings out again the connection between teaching and indoctrination. 'Indoctrination' is inappropriate unless the agent is teaching. This rules out chance happenings, unconscious influence, and events over which the agent has no control: indoctrination involves intention. However, because of the pejorative nature of 'indoctrination', the agent is not the best judge of what he is doing.

Indoctrination and beliefs

The indoctrinator teaches with the intention that the pupil or pupils *believe* P. This aspect brings home the point that indoctrination is concerned with beliefs. Crittenden (1968) found in his search of several dictionaries that their one point of agreement was that all implied that 'indoctrination' is inappropriate in reference to behaviour. Expressions such as 'indoctrinated to clean their teeth', 'indoctrinated to salute the flag', 'indoctrinated with etiquette' are a misuse of the term. Where behaviour is uppermost, the term 'conditioning' or 'training' is more normally used. (See the discussion of conditioning in chapter 5.)

Indoctrination is concerned with propositional knowledge (knowing *that*), with statements which can be true or false. When the charge of indoctrination is made it is appropriate to ask what beliefs are involved.

This distinction can help in the solution of the problem of the moral training of the young child. This involves the inculcation of habits rather than beliefs and the term 'indoctrination' is not appropriate. In so far as morality becomes a matter of beliefs ('because it is your duty', 'because God wills it'), the intention criterion must come into play: is this a step towards evidentially held beliefs or is it the beginning of the inculcation of one set of beliefs? In the latter case, the term 'indoctrination' becomes appropriate.

Indoctrination and evidence

I have argued that the indoctrinator intends that the pupil believe P 'regardless of the evidence'. In full-blown cases of intention, this captures very well the difference between the indoctrinator and the educator. For the educator, the beliefs are always secondary to the evidence: he wants his students to end up with whatever beliefs the evidence demands. He is concerned with methods of assessing data, standards of accuracy, and validity of reasoning. The answers are subsidiary to the methods of gaining answers. The indoctrinator, however, is typically most concerned with the imparting of the beliefs: these are what he strives to hand on. It is the evidence that is of subsidiary importance. As I have argued earlier, the indoctrinator will himself make use of evidence, logic, and proof—but it is a *use of*, in order to further his aim: the beliefs are more important than the evidence.

The cavalier treatment of evidence is exemplified most obviously in those systems which are called ideologies. Corbett (1965, pp. 121-3) has documented this aspect of Marxism. In Marxist social theory, the proletariat (wage earners) is seen as an oppressed class, growing poorer until it inevitably spear-heads revolution. When the facts turn out otherwise, the claim is not denied but simply reinterpreted. When it is established that the workers are getting richer not poorer, the Marxist answers that *relatively* they are getting poorer. When it is suggested that in some countries workers are not oppressed, the reply is that they are oppressed in more subtle ways. Remark that the peasants, not the proletariat, have spear-headed revolution, and the 'proletariat' is redefined as 'the workers and peasants'.

Roman Catholicism, another 'ideological' system, adopts similar tactics. The claim is made that the Church cannot make a mistake about faith or morals and cannot therefore change a ruling on these matters. Point to an obvious change (usury was once condemned and is now accepted) and the reply is either that this was not a matter of morals or that the teaching did not change: something else changed (the nature of money). The Pope is infallible. Pius IX condemned the proposition that men are free to worship according to their conscience; Vatican II affirmed this freedom. Solution: Pius IX was not being infallible on this matter. The result is that evidence can never go against the claim: *any* evidence is compatible with the claim.

Examples of ideological thinking can also be found within psychology. A strict behaviourist asserts that 'all learning occurs by means of reinforcement' and means to assert something quite significant. Point out that a child seems to learn some words solely by imitation and the reply is that the child is being reinforced 'automatically'. Indicate that we frequently keep on at a task just because it is hard to solve, and the behaviourist answers that care in problem solving is 'self-reinforcing' (Chomsky, 1959, p. 37). In due course, the term 'reinforcement' becomes so attenuated that the original claim is empty. The behaviourist (like the Marxist or Catholic) can *always* sustain his case by rewriting it to suit the evidence or by reinterpreting the evidence so that the case remains untouched.

In an ideology, the claims are more important than the evidence. Small wonder that when an ideology is being taught, evidence plays only a minor role. We do associate indoctrination with ideologies and with good reason. The misuse (not necessarily the suppression or denial) of evidence is one of the main reasons why this is so.

Criticism of the evidence criterion

If it is granted that the manner in which ideologies use evidence is to be deplored, the question can be raised as to the role of evidence in other matters. The following criticisms might be made of the attempt to link 'indoctrination' so closely with the concept of 'evidence'.

1   The connection can be criticized on the grounds that the concept of evidence finds its place in empirical claims. The notion of evidence is inappropriate for example in mathematics and morality. Here we seek for logical argument, deductive proof, and good reasons. We do not demand evidence. Hence, the argument runs, my analysis of indoctrination cannot cover cases where proof or good reasons rather than evidence are required.

Two strategies are open to us:

i   We can go along with this and assert that indoctrination *is* restricted to factual claims about the world and that where evidence is inappropriate, the notion of indoctrination is also out of place. Hence we could not talk of indoctrinating mathematics or morals. This reply works rather well for mathematics which is a self-contained system of axioms and demonstrations. For morals, it works to some extent: morals are concerned with behaviour and to that extent 'indoctrination' is not apposite. On the other hand, many of the reasons given for a moral decision are empirical claims ('this will injure him') and the evidence criterion *is* appropriate. However, it is almost certainly true that ultimately there is a gap between facts and values: moral reasoning has a style and validity of its own and evidence is only partly a cogent factor (people can agree on the evidence and still *logically* disagree about what is to be done). The handing on of moral points of view seems to be open to the charge of indoctrination even though 'evidence' does not seem to fit.

ii   A second possible strategy is that used by Scheffler in his discussion of the evidence criterion in analyses of 'know' (Scheffler, 1965, p. 59). The objection can be met, he suggests, by construing 'evidence' as including proofs and reasons in the areas in which these are more appropriate than evidence in the strict sense. A person has adequate evidence for Q when he has good reasons for believing Q. What 'good reasons' consist of will vary with the subject concerned.

2 It might also be objected by one of strong philosophical bent that evidence cannot be had for any proposition and that the demand that people hold their beliefs on the basis of evidence is an unrealistic one. This objection might be stated in the following ways. (i) The demand that a belief be based on evidence leads to an infinite regress: for we must have adequate evidence for accepting the evidence, etc., etc.: i.e. we believe P because of Z, Z because of Y, Y because of X, and so on. (ii) Empirical propositions are at best *probable*: there is no certainty in any knowledge which is gained by means of induction.

This is not the place to enter into the philosophical justification of knowledge itself. Nor is it necessary. What we are interested in is an investigation of an educational problem and this sets limits which entitle us to avoid the deeper issue. Machan (1970, p. 262) has argued for an epistemology of education and although some of his assertions are open to serious question he does stress that education requires an account of the evolutionary nature of human knowledge. In brief, what is vitally necessary is some understanding of what can be legitimately taught at any particular stage in history. In our terms, we need some convention, according to which we can meaningfully say that teaching X was not indoctrination last century, but is today. We want, further, a criterion which as far as possible is neutral towards the various philosophical positions. If one's account of indoctrination rests on a particular view of reality and knowledge, it will be open for others to reject it if they hold a different metaphysical or epistemological view.

Evidence and the schools

It would be pretentious to suppose that in a book of this nature I could map out anything approximating to an 'epistemology of education' but something has to be said or else the criterion of evidence will not be useful in the analysis of 'indoctrination'.

I would argue that schools are concerned not so much with 'truth' (over which men differ philosophically and factually) but with what is 'established' by those who are regarded as competent in the area in question. This does not mean that the man in the street has no part to play at all. He plays his role by the acceptance of certain experts as experts. A proposition in chemistry is supported by evidence if those who study chemistry accept this evidence; the layman's acceptance of such men as experts justifies his acceptance of their authority and justifies the teacher's teaching even if he himself is not in a position to evaluate the evidence. However, if the biologists were to agree that biological warfare is militarily justified, this would not constitute evidence since they are not regarded as experts in *that*. That is to say, evidence is related to consensus, although truth is not.

It might be objected at this point that if my analysis is accepted the classroom teacher cannot safely teach anything. Even in mathematics or physics there are controversies on the boundaries of the discipline, and in subjects such as history and literature, there are always current and well-known disputes. The teacher may not be aware of these or, if he is, may judge that they are too subtle for the age or intelligence of those he is concerned with. In so far as a dispute belongs only to the higher reaches of the subject, the teacher cannot be held responsible for not conveying it. He neither desires nor foresees that the pupils will believe regardless of the evidence, and he cannot be accused of indoctrinating.

When the doubt is integral to the study even at the level the teacher is concerned with, it could be argued that the teacher *should* be aware of it. However, there is so much that a teacher ideally 'should' be familiar with that we are inclined to be cautious about demanding such requirements on pain of moral fault.

The point being made is this: while many things are desirable in teaching, criticisms such as 'you are indoctrinating him' cannot rest on these idealistic requirements. They must be based on minimal demands. I would assert therefore that the teacher at any level is at least bound to take account of those matters in which the doubtful validity of the evidence is common knowledge in the community: political, social, and religious statements are doubtful in this sense. Indoctrination is most likely to occur in these areas.

Intention and motive

A brief discussion of motive is necessary for four reasons: (i) the possession of a good motive does not excuse one from the charge of indoctrination; (ii) the fact that a particular teacher has a motive for indoctrinating does not entitle us to say that he is indoctrinating; (iii) however, the possession of a motive is strongly suggestive of the possibility of indoctrination and the teacher with such a motive should take particular care; and (iv) it is unlikely that a person is indoctrinating if he has no conceivable motive for doing so.

I have attempted to distinguish intention from motive by suggesting that intention specifies what the teacher is doing, motive explains why he is doing it. There are cases in which this distinction will not hold up and some would argue that the logical distinction cannot be sustained. Nevertheless, it is a useful distinction in the analysis of indoctrination.

Wilson (1966, pp. 391-2) confuses the two. He argues that the teacher's aim (intention) cannot be the criterion of indoctrination since a person might think that it is right to indoctrinate children with certain myths in order to give them security, 'and however liberal the aim or intention, it would still be indoctrination'. On my distinction, this is a misguided objection. It is clear that what the teacher intends is that these myths be believed. The motive (security) is irrelevant to the charge of indoctrination. Whether this teacher was indoctrinating or not would depend not on his motive for propounding the myths but on the nature of the myths. There is little likelihood of the child growing up with the belief that his father can cope with every problem in the world. Nor is the child likely to cling forever to a belief in Father Christmas. Since the teacher neither intends nor foresees that there will be any long-term effect on the child's mind, the charge of indoctrination is not appropriate. On the other hand, unscientific notions about sex, dogmatic views of religion, and prejudices about social position are likely to persist and be inimical to the later consideration of evidence. If one taught these 'myths', with the knowledge of their doubtful status, he would be indoctrinating. The motive for propounding the myths has no effect on the charge of indoctrination.

Holbrook (1963, p. 111), writing about the teaching of religion in universities, protests against the tendency for other faculty members to charge professors of religion with indoctrinating without providing any warrant for the charge. The charge, he argues, is frequently gratuitous 'since suspicion of motive is neither evidence nor proof of the charge'. This is certainly correct, although a subject like religion is suspect because it is not clear what else the teacher can intend other than belief or commitment. Nevertheless, something more is required for sheeting home the charge of indoctrination than the fact that the teacher has a motive.

An interesting illustration of this is provided by an actual case (*A.A.U.P. Bulletin*, 1967, pp. 278-91). The administration of a university hired a sociology professor, knowing that he had strong Marxist sympathies. He was subsequently dismissed on the following grounds: (i) Marx was the only reading prescribed for his courses; (ii) his examinations covered only polemical questions; and (iii) he had announced his intention to continue to teach in this manner. The administration concluded with some justification that he was indoctrinating. The reader will notice how the criteria I outlined are operating, (i) he had a motive (he was a Marxist); (ii) his style of teaching gave evidence of an intention (weak sense, at least); and (iii) he admitted an intention (strong sense).

We might profitably compare this case with two hypothetical cases. Suppose another Marxist were to give fair consideration to other social theorists: the motive would not be grounds for assuming an indoctrinating intention. What about a non-Marxist who also restricted his reading list to Marx on the grounds that he had found this the best way to launch into a discussion of social theory: in the absence of any motive for indoctrinating Marxism, we might accept that no reprehensible intention was involved.

So, in actual cases in which indoctrination is alleged, the application of the intention criterion will require skill. Nevertheless, it is argued, the intention of the teacher is the crucial factor.

Some cases

Any analysis of indoctrination must take account of cases which actually occur in an educational setting. It must clearly cover those cases which are recognized as indoctrination, must exclude those which we do not want to label indoctrination, and provide a way of handling the doubtful cases in a consistent and useful manner.

1 Cases which are clearly indoctrination:

    a Teaching an ideology as if it were the only one with any claim to rationality.

    b Teaching, as if they are certain, propositions which the teacher knows are uncertain.

    c Teaching propositions which the teacher knows to be false.

2 Cases which may seem like indoctrination but which are not:

    a Teaching young children acceptable behaviour.

    b Teaching facts (the tables, or Latin verbs) by rote.

    c Influencing the child unconsciously.

3 Problematic cases:

    a Inculcating beliefs which the teacher believes are certain but which are substantially disputed.

b Teaching any subject without due concern for understanding.

On the criterion I have put forward, all cases under 1 are adequately covered. The teacher intends fixed beliefs, in the strong sense. If he denies such an intention, he can be shown that it is an area of doubt and uncertainty (at the very least) and that what he is doing is sure to result in fixed beliefs. Once alerted, he can foresee the outcome and 'indoctrination' is appropriate. A rough guide to his intention will often be the attitude he takes towards one who rejects these beliefs. If this rejection is seen as a failure, a rejection of all he has taught, he has been indoctrinating.

Case 2a is ruled out: beliefs and evidence are not relevant to this early training and the question of indoctrination does not arise. Case 2b is excluded since there is little chance of the tables or verbs impairing the child's later assessment of evidence ('evidence' is not really relevant to things like tables or verbs anyway). Since there are no consequences liable for moral review, intention does not arise as an issue. Case 2c is ruled out because unconscious influences are (by definition) not intentional.

Case 3a is a case of indoctrination if the teacher knows that the beliefs are disputed: he foresees that what he is teaching is likely to be believed despite the fact that the evidence is inconclusive. Case 3b might be indoctrination if (i) there were positive intent to make the child incapable of impartial appraisal of the subject or (ii) non-rational methods were so consistently used as to lead to contempt for the evidence. The charge could always be rebutted by showing that both (i) there was no intention (strong sense); this might be done by showing there was no motive; and (ii) in the main, rational methods were used.

This line of defence is open also to the busy teacher who must often neglect to give reasons: the overall intention is the key.

In this way there is provision for a distinction of content on the grounds of whether fixed beliefs are more or less appropriate. There is also scope for the realization that dogmatic teaching even of an exact science can warp the students' thought.

Conclusion

'Indoctrination' implies a pejorative judgment on a teaching situation. It suggests that someone is taking advantage of a privileged role to influence those under his charge in a manner which is likely to distort their ability to assess the evidence on its own merit. The positive intention to bring about this state of mind is sufficient for the application of the term to his teaching, even if he should fail in his task: 'indoctrination' is both a task and an achievement word. Such a desire is not necessary, however, if it is foreseen that this state of mind is likely as a result of what is being done. In all cases, some action must be intentional in the strong sense. A person cannot indoctrinate if he is not doing anything intentional at all: one cannot indoctrinate by omission. One can be held responsible for omissions, but 'indoctrination' is not an appropriate term for them.

Intentions are paramount but content and method are important. From a consideration of method, an observer can detect the intention to indoctrinate. Content is important because not all content is equally susceptible to indoctrination. Drill in Latin verbs is far less likely than drill in patriotic sentiments to result in 'beliefs regardless of the evidence'. Doctrines in the sense of ideologies are not essential to the concept but they often provide the motive for indoctrination. Because we find it difficult to imagine a motive for indoctrinating physics we tend to exclude the teaching of such subjects from indoctrination. I have argued that the concept can include them, but a motive is needed to explain why anyone would want to indoctrinate them.

4
Indoctrination and education

According to my account of 'indoctrination' there are few conceptual limits to the subject matter that can be indoctrinated. It is clear, however, that in fact indoctrination is most likely to occur in the areas of morals, religion, and politics, for these are matters upon which informed people differ. Yet most of us think it essential that children be introduced to a set of moral values, a political system, and a religious tradition. This means that the sincere educator whether he is a parent or a teacher faces a dilemma. On one hand, he believes it to be desirable that the children yield to the demands of a moral order, are informed about and committed to a form of social life, and are able in some degree to grapple with questions which have characteristically been described as religious. On the other hand, he is presumably concerned with the ethical problem of indoctrination and knows well from his observations and experience that what passes for education in these areas is frequently indoctrination in its fullest sense.

Negative education

Faced with this dilemma, a number of theorists have argued

that all moral, religious, and political training should be delayed until such time as the child's rationality has developed to such an extent that he can evaluate the various positions for himself and come to the conclusions which he judges to be most reasonable. There are reasons for thinking that this conclusion is unacceptable and even incoherent.

1 It is simply not the case that an avoidance of moral training, for example, is in any way a method of avoiding influencing the child morally. As Nell (1969, pp. 8-9) has pointed out in a criticism of Rousseau, any policy of permissiveness can be described in more than one way. On the face of it, a permissive approach is a policy of freedom. A child who is not taught rules of etiquette, then, is being released from the imposition of custom. However, an alternative description is that the child is being denied the skills necessary for his social living: his freedom is being inhibited, not fostered. As Nell points out, a decision not to teach certain skills or attitudes does not ensure that the child will develop naturally. It may rather ensure that in some area he will not be able to develop at all. Parents do not avoid the responsibility for forming their children's characters simply because they choose to describe their methods as *negative*; the same methods can also be described as *positive* education in another direction.

This argument is most cogent in the area of moral and social development. It can, however, be generalized to some extent to include matters of religion and politics. To choose not to teach the child to pray is still to make a choice. This choice, like the choice of permissiveness in etiquette, can be justified, but the point I am making is that it needs justification just as much as the choice to insist on table manners or evening prayers. To be 'permissive'

69

in such matters is not to avoid a value commitment; it is to make a different value commitment.

2 The second objection to 'negative education' is that rationality is not an all-or-nothing affair. Children do not become rational at the age of eleven or fifteen. Rationality is not a development in the sense that puberty is. It is the result of experiences of various sorts and the child's reactions to these experiences. It is the outcome of social living, a common language, and an inheritance of concepts and attitudes handed down in some tradition. To deny to the child experiences of moral dilemmas and religious problems is *by that fact* to stunt his rationality. To wait for moral reasoning before beginning moral training is like waiting for the child to compose a sonata before beginning his musical education.

This is the great dilemma of education: how can educators hand on traditions in which rationality is defined, without stunting the rationality of the child in the process? To put it another way: how can we educate (i.e. pass on forms of thought we value) without indoctrination? Two subsidiary questions are involved here: (i) what form should training take once the child is regarded as educable and (ii) what should be done in those early years when habits are being formed and rationality is but a tender bud?

In trying to come to grips with this problem I shall concentrate on religion. It is not possible in a short book to do justice to morals, religion, and politics. Much remains to be done in each of these areas, and once we are fully aware of the problem of indoctrination many years of exciting and important thinking and research lie open. Even in religion, I cannot hope to provide any firm conclusions. The most that I can hope for is that some fruitful ideas may emerge from which those interested in religious education can develop practical procedures for religious education as opposed to religious indoctrination.

Morals and politics

Before concentrating on religious education, however, I want to mention some very promising work in the area of morals which is opening up the possibility of a form of moral education to replace the moral indoctrination which in the past has been so typical and, by all accounts, so conspicuously unsuccessful. At the Farmington Trust Unit at Oxford, John Wilson and his associates are working on programmes of moral education which take into account the problem of indoctrination. This project incorporates philosophical insights into the nature of morals, psychological evidence related to moral development, and sociological evidence related to the influences of home, peers, church, and school in developing moral character (Wilson, Williams, Sugarman, 1967). Their basic point of view, if I can be so rash as to summarize it, is that attempts to hand on moral codes of any sort are species of indoctrination and are to be deprecated. What must be done, then, is to teach children to be rational about morals, as about history, mathematics, and home financing. They argue that there is a style of moral argument just as there is a style of mathematical argument. There are rules for playing the moral game and regardless of what moral principles are in fact held a person must obey these rules if he is to be thinking morally at all. These *procedural rules*, which of course have still to be worked out fully, will constitute the core of a programme of moral education. Such a programme cannot, they would argue, be

called indoctrination since its whole purpose is to encourage children to weight the evidence, consider the consequences, and so on, all of which is the very antithesis of
indoctrination as we have defined it.

The work of Kohlberg and his associates at Harvard has
basically similar aims although it does not so clearly
emerge from a concern to avoid indoctrination. The Harvard team, extending the work of Piaget but influenced also
by philosophical speculation on the nature of morality,
have identified a number of stages of moral thinking
through which children pass. They claim that these are
culture-neutral and quite independent of the particular content of the morality in question. In the area of moral
education as distinct from the descriptive side of developmental psychology, they are involved in work on classroom intervention which aims at raising the quality of the
children's moral thinking. Once again, as with the work
of Wilson at Oxford, there is the possibility of a form of
moral education which operates on the quality of the
student's thinking rather than on the specific content of his
moral beliefs (Kohlberg, 1963, 1966, 1968, 1969).

Both of these projects involve interesting possibilities
for moral education and may, to some extent, provide
a practical way out of the educator's dilemma.

In the area of politics, not so much is being done. In
the United States, philosophers of education have always
been interested in the role of the school in political matters and, as we have mentioned already, the literature on
indoctrination there has been concerned with the role of
the school in imparting political values. After a period in
which this concern lay fallow, there has been a recent re-
vival of interest in the problem under the heading of
'neutrality'. On the philosophical level, this has poten-

tial for developing into a worthwhile and stimulating topic (Ennis, 1959; Hoffman, 1964; McClellan, 1968; Eckstein, 1969; Ennis, 1969). What needs to be done, as in the projects on moral education, is for this activity to be combined with empirical studies of how children develop political ideas (e.g. Hess and Torney, 1968) and the part played by various institutions in the political education of the young. Heater's book (1969) represents another attempt by a number of writers to argue for a form of political *education* which avoids indoctrination on one hand, and infertile fact-grubbing on the other.

One of the signs that the study of education is coming of age is that, from the activities of philosophers, psychologists, and sociologists on issues where indoctrination is of concern, there is slowly emerging a theory of education to guide teachers in these important areas of educational practice (Hirst, 1966).

But that is to digress. In the remainder of this chapter I want to relate our discussion of indoctrination to the teaching of religion.

Religion

In posing the dilemma early in this chapter I asked: how is it possible to hand on forms of thought we believe to be valuable without at the same time limiting the child's rationality? I also suggested that this question involves two subsidiary questions: (i) what form should training take once the child has reached an educable age (ii) what should be done in the early years when habits are being formed, prior to the flowering of reason? This dilemma is, of course, most acute in those domains of life where the evidence is inconclusive, where equally knowledgeable and sincere men differ, and where (sadly) people are prone to hold to their views tenaciously regardless of evidence or argument.

Religion is a prime (perhaps *the* prime) example of such a domain. It is abundantly clear that many religious statements are meant to be taken as factually true. They may involve a special use of language, even metaphor, but they are not meant to be read purely as poetry. The claim is that in some sense these statements are true. There is no need to document the claim that throughout the centuries Christians have meant their theological statements to be taken rather literally. The various theological controversies and the persecution of dissidents indicate that theological statements were intended to be precise and meaningful. It would be a mistake to imagine that this has changed in orthodox religious circles: 'heresy' is still an appropriate term and for being condemned as a heretic, punishments are meted out. References could be given to responsible sources, Catholic and Protestant, in which the 'truths' to be believed are categorically stated. To cite such references would be to labour the obvious. Christian teachers of all persuasions are expected to teach for belief in certain propositions, the propositions varying from sect to sect.

It is clear that such teaching is indoctrination because whatever the particular proposition the evidence for it is inconclusive: it is rejected by other competent authorities. That all religious propositions are doubtful in this sense is sufficient to indicate that teaching for belief in them is always indoctrination. But we can go even further: we can show that at least some of these propositions are false.

i   Some of the 'truths' taught are contradictory: at least one must be false.

ii   Within any Church, important changes occur in what is taught.

These points are often made by those who want to show that belief in the inerrancy of the Bible or the infallibility of the Church is mistaken. There is no need to make such a strong point here. It is sufficient to indicate that the 'truths' presented for acceptance in one age are often changed in the next, as the weight of evidence becomes massive. Religious apologists go to great lengths to show 'consistency', however bizarre the notion of consistency. However, this strategy does not affect the argument being developed here as two examples suggest. Churches persisted in condemning evolution despite a growing body of scientific evidence in its favour. Some sects and individuals continue to condemn it even today when the basic evidence is conclusive. The Roman Catholic Church condemned usury in a most solemn manner even after it had gained general acceptance: it no longer does so. This shows that at one time people were taught to hold firmly to *what was then disputed* and is now regarded as false even by the churchmen themselves.

The issue, then, can be summed up in the following way:

1 Indoctrination is the teaching of any subject matter with the intention that it be believed regardless of the evidence.

2 Indoctrination, so defined, is morally reprehensible.

3 Religious propositions are meant to be true, but the evidence for all of them is inconclusive and some of them are false. (That we cannot identify which ones are false does not affect the argument.)

4 If the parent or teacher teaches them with the intention that they be believed, he indoctrinates.

5 It is difficult to see what else the teacher of religion could intend.

6 Indoctrination is inevitable if religion is taught.

75

7   The teaching of religion is an immoral activity.

In the face of this argument, ways of avoiding indoc-trination seem limited. Four possible escape routes seem available: (i) cease teaching religion altogether; (ii) delay all teaching of religion until the child is old enough to investigate it without the parent-child or teacher-pupil relationship having its obvious effect; (iii) remove the pro-positional element of religion, making it simply 'a stance towards the world' and so rendering 'indoctrination' an inappropriate term; (iv) change the method and/or content so radically that it cannot be said that the teacher intends the pupils to hold beliefs regardless of the evidence.

In a Christian culture strategies (i) and (ii) are unlikely to be accepted and, as I argued earlier, (ii) is probably pedagogically unsound. Only (iii) and (iv) seem viable and these will be considered in the succeeding sections.

Religion and indoctrination

I have argued that religious statements are doubtful in that the evidence for them is inconclusive. Contemporary philo-sophical discussion of religion has, however, cast over religious statements a doubt of a more radical sort. In-fluenced by logical positivism philosophers have argued that since religious statements are neither verifiable nor falsi-fiable, they are not real statements at all. They do not assert anything and hence can be neither true nor false.

As a result of this criticism a whole literature has de-veloped in which the application of the principles of veri-fication and falsification to religion have been argued. This debate has resulted in two significant outcomes: (i) It has been generally conceded, that as a theory of *meaning*, the view of the positivists was arbitrary and extreme. It rendered scientific theories meaningless and, when applied to itself, the verification theory itself became meaningless. That is to say, the claim that 'all meaningful synthetic statements must be verifiable in experience' was not itself open to such verification. (ii) There remains, however, a powerful weapon against self-deception and wishful thinking. Granted that a claim such as 'Jesus was the Son of God' can be accepted as meaningful, we are surely entitled to ask, 'what evidence is there for it?' or 'what reason have we to think that it is true?'

As a result of these attacks on the meaningfulness of religious statements, we are left with a legacy that is significant for the discussion of indoctrination. The criticism of religious statements ceases to be based on a doctrinaire view of meaning and becomes instead founded on the general commitment to rationality. For who, without contracting out of rationality altogether, could possibly claim that we ought to believe what we do not have good reason to believe?

Critics of religion push home their advantage by arguing that not only are religious people in disagreement about what is to be believed but also about what would count for or against their diverse beliefs. Religion is not simply a matter of dispute; it is a matter of totally subjective dispute. It not only involves commitment but presupposes non-rational commitment.

If this case is sustained, *all* forms of religious teaching are indoctrination. It is not a matter of taking care to avoid indoctrination while teaching religion. For there is no way of specifying what taking care means. We can tell people to take care in climbing a mountain or solving a mathematical problem because in these activities there are certain standard procedures to be followed. There is no point in telling people to take care in how they fall from an aeroplane: we cannot in any way specify what taking care means in this context. And so, in discussing religious teaching this argument leads us to say that whatever we do, we must be indoctrinating. For we avoid indoctrination when teaching history or philosophy by making available to our students the objective standards and critical methods by which we and the text-books can be shown to be mistaken. In religion, the argument runs, there are no objective standards and no critical methods and hence we cannot (logically, cannot) avoid indoctrination.

There is no doubt that this is a powerful argument. Some religious people and even religious philosophers, especially of the 'existential' variety, give added cogency to it by agreeing on the basic subjectivity of religious belief. They ought to be aware that on this view religious education becomes impossible. Of course, there may be a place for commitment in religion and in other matters but if it is the ground-rock of religious belief, religion is removed from rational dialogue, and any notion of critical standards disappears. It becomes impossible to withstand the conclusion that religion has no place in education.

I am, therefore, in an invidious position. On the one hand I am forced to fight off the attacks of those who argue that, since they are convinced of the truth of their religious beliefs, they are entitled to teach them to their children as true. On the other hand, I am assailed by those who argue that, since there is no religious knowledge but only religious belief, no form of religious teaching can be legitimate. I have already argued against the former view on the grounds that the absence of religious agreement precludes religious belief being taught as true. What remains to be done is to sketch an argument for the position that the fact of religious disagreement does not preclude the possibility that religion is a form of knowledge with its own standards and procedures. In the section which follows, I attempt to construct the outlines of such a case.

Religion as a form of knowledge

The easiest way of approaching this issue is to consider what a person might mean when he says he has a religious problem. If religious beliefs are completely subjective, it is not very clear what a religious problem is. Yet people do have, or claim to have, religious problems. Basically these involve questions of belief (Is there a God?), questions of attitude towards the world (What is the meaning of life?), moral questions (Must I pay my taxes?), questions of personal or social ideals (Should I devote myself to the poor?), and questions of worship (Should I pray?). Some of these questions are not uniquely religious. A person can have a moral problem without having a religious problem and a man can explore his ideals without placing them in a religious context, and so on. The point is, however, that when such questions are seen as religious questions they are viewed in a context which includes the other questions. If a person says he has a religious problem and then states a moral problem, he is seeking a solution in terms of a distinctive point of view about duties, sanctions, and a law-giver. A religious question, then, is a question of the sort given above, seen in relation to these other sorts of questions. It is this interrelationship which converts a moral question into a religious question.

Many philosophers have in recent times attempted to reduce all religious questions to one or other of these categories. Religion becomes identical with morality, social values, or attitudes towards life. It seems unlikely that any of these reductions can in fact be sustained. I would go further and assert that the logically basic questions are those which are most frequently reduced or neglected— the questions of belief. If a person has a problem about ideals and does not in any way care about answers to questions about beliefs, his problem ceases to be a religious problem. Basic to religion is a set of beliefs about God, his relationship to the world, and the attitude He would have us take towards Himself, the world, and ourselves. The indoctrination issue cannot be solved by saying that religion has nothing to do with beliefs. We have to face the problem of how these beliefs might be justified. For even if we feel that we do not need to face this question ourselves, it remains a crucial one if we want to educate others.

For centuries attempts have been made to demonstrate basic beliefs by means of rational argument. Proofs have been devised for the existence of God, the spirituality of the soul, and immortality. These arguments have been criticized and defended, demolished and amended right up to our own day. It would be an overstatement to suggest that these arguments have given us firm knowledge which justifies our teaching the conclusions to the young. It would be equally wrong to suggest that these arguments have been pointless or that there are no 'accepted standards' for the debate. If this were so, why have philosophers tried to amend the arguments? One does not amend unless the criticism has been accepted and the acceptance of criticism implies shared standards. It may be the case that it is rare for a person to believe or disbelieve on the basis of these 'proofs' alone but this is not the point. The point here is that these arguments are seriously entertained, their objective standards are generally accepted. We have the beginnings of a form of religious knowledge. Certainly, it could not be said that a teacher who carefully discussed these proofs with his class, and gave fair consideration to opposing arguments, *must* be indoctrinating.

It might be said that he would not be teaching religion either; he would be teaching philosophy of religion. This really is the great problem. 'Teaching religion' as it is normally understood suggests the imparting of religious doctrines in such a way that the pupil accepts them as true. Many teachers of religion would think they had failed unless firm belief was the outcome. Such teaching clearly merits the title of indoctrination. Only if we can break up religion into its component parts and specify the criteria for truth and falsity have we any hope of justifying the teaching of religion at all. The philosophical justification of basic religious beliefs is one element in the religious tradition and it holds some hope for setting religious education on a firm basis.

Religious doctrines, especially those of Christianity, depend on historical or allegedly historical events. Of course they are not identical with historical events since, if they were, they would be part of historical knowledge simply and there would be no need to call them religious (except in the trivial sense in which the Crusades are religious history). Some have argued a stronger view than this and have suggested that historical scholarship is irrelevant to religious belief. Basil Mitchell has shown that if a religion is rooted in history, historical considerations cannot be *irrelevant*. If Jesus did not die on a cross (historical event) then much of Christian theology is mistaken (Mitchell, 1969). Mitchell also goes on to argue that, in other more positive ways, the discussion of the Scriptures, for example, can be a rational matter not too different from the activities of historians dealing with the secular literature of Plato (Mitchell, p. 193). Once again, it is not necessary to argue that all are agreed on the facts and their interpretation. Clearly, they are not. It is sufficient to show that something rational can go on, that two people can differ over the historical elements of Christianity without just agreeing to differ. Dispute over the Resurrection, for example, can be conducted rationally. Both sides can accept the basic data, that something happened to the disciples, and can go on to argue what interpretation must be placed on the data in order to make sense of it. This may not be pure historical scholarship since the hypothesis 'a dead man came to life' is not one which historians customarily postulate. Nevertheless, the activity is not radically different. There is a body of evidence and some critical standards. In this way, too, religion can be justified as a form of knowledge.

In Christianity, appeal is also made to the notion of revelation. God has revealed himself, or is revealing himself to men. The justification of particular beliefs takes place by reference to a community of believers, and a tradition in which the revelatory experience is distilled for its meaning and relevance. A great deal of theology is devoted to this type of activity. The argument that this activity provides its own standards of judgments works well enough if we are concerned with the meaning of concepts. Terms such as worship, sin, and salvation are defined and elaborated within a tradition and understanding them involves mastering this tradition. However, this activity can tell us nothing about the truth of the propositions in which the concepts are used. For example, a study of the Christian tradition can tell us what is meant by 'Jesus is the Saviour' but it seems powerless to tell us whether He was the Saviour.

At this point the tendency of religious people (even philosophers) is to speak of faith, based on some form of religious experience. The outsider cannot deny that such things are involved in the notion of religion nor can he deny *a priori* that people have such experiences. The difficulty is, however, that we find it hard to distinguish a *religious* experience from other kinds of experience and faith from delusion. At any rate, a strongly subjective element is involved, by definition, and the demand for public justification seems pointless.

What can be demanded, however, is that alternative hypotheses be considered (e.g. perhaps Jesus was not the Saviour but the apostles thought He was) and that alternative systems (which all have their equivalent of the 'leap of faith') be given fair treatment. Other religions and semi-religions have their sets of concepts and style of arguing and these should be examined. For there is a sense in which all bodies of knowledge, even an empirical science, are *sui generis* (see Coulson, 1966). Ultimately, the test must be how well they accord with human experience. When the educator has made available the alternative schemes, the final judgment must be left to the student.

Religion is a messy area. That I have admitted. But it is not so messy that no critical standards can be indentified. The onus is on everyone who attempts to teach religion to show what criteria he regards as significant and what considerations he would accept as counting against his statements. The person who accepts that logical argument can demonstrate the existence of God is bound to abide by the students' conviction that the arguments are invalid and that God does not exist. The tendency of many teachers of religion, however, is to glide from one mode of justification to another so that if one fails, another takes up the slack. In this form of teaching, it is fair to say that the teacher wants belief 'regardless of the evidence' and 'indoctrination' is appropriate.

Having established some sort of case for the position that religion need not be completely subjective, I want to go on to suggest in very broad terms some possible approaches to the teaching of religion which would avoid being species of indoctrination.

I have already mentioned the multi-tiered doubt concerning religious statements. There is doubt whether a particular proposition is true, whether any religious propositions are true, and whether religious propositions are even meaningful. These levels of doubt make it extremely difficult to discuss methods of teaching religion. For a method suggested by a modern theologian or philosopher may be consistent with his view of religion but not acceptable to others with a more orthodox view. In searching for possible ways of teaching religion without indoctrination it is necessary to sift those which rely on a particular theory of religious language from those which, even if derived from it, are not antipathetic to the other views. This is not to say that the methods to be suggested will be welcomed equally by all schools of thought but only that they seem to escape the stigma of indoctrination. A religionist who cannot accept any of these methods as adequate is challenged to produce one that is acceptable and not subject to the charge of indoctrination.

Because I am concerned with an educational issue, the philosophical and theological views have been touched only lightly in the following pages. However, because some of the methods have philosophical or theological roots, it has been necessary to mention them in passing.

Religion and doubt

An obvious way out of the dilemma is to advocate that there be no teaching *of* religion but only teaching *about* religion. The children will be told what others believe but will not themselves be asked to believe. Advocates of religious education have frequently deprecated such an approach because they regard their own faith as being of great significance and insist that commitment is an essential factor in religion. They, therefore, seem to demand that indoctrination take place. I have tried to argue that this is not an acceptable gambit: indoctrination is to be ruled out in religious as in all other matters.

There is, however, a genuine problem here as Wilson (1970, p. 3) has shown. He points out that we could teach people *about* mathematics or science by teaching them the history or sociology of these fields but this would not constitute mathematical or scientific education. Similarly, he argues, if a form of religious education is to be developed it will have to be one which leads the children into an understanding of what religion is all about. Comparative religion and that sort of thing cannot, he believes, constitute the core of religious education, although he admits (p. 11) that these may be a worthwhile adjunct to religious education.

Perhaps we can move a step further by considering a suggestion made by Stanley (1953, ch. 7) in a context unrelated to religion. He argues that in a society which is pluralistic and confused about its values and goals the best that the school can do as a form of political education is to study this confusion itself. In this way, the study can be factual yet not avoid the value questions that are part of political life. It is clear that in religion in general and in the individual denominations there is today a good deal of confusion. The school could focus its educational programme on this confusion either in general or in a particular sect. Teacher and class could investigate together the state of the Church: its historical foundations and claims, qualifications that have been made in them, various modern theological views, attacks from within and without. The Protestant who wants to centre instruction on the Bible could discuss its history, the various interpretations, scholarly opinions on its authenticity, comparison with the sacred books of other religions etc. The Catholic could study the conciliar and papal statements on all issues, current theological conflicts, liturgical disputes, and the like.

Indoctrination would be avoided if the teacher, regardless of his own commitment, taught with the intention that the pupils form their own conclusions on the basis of evidence. At the same time it would not be simply a matter of describing controversies but of entering into them in some way, and gaining an understanding of what they are all about. This kind of approach is one possible answer to the problem of religious education.

Culture, language, and symbols

A number of modern theologians, while holding that theological propositions are statements about a supernatural order, insist that the propositions themselves are culture-bound. They reflect the presuppositions of the age in which they were formulated. If it is true that language enshrines a cultural outlook and religious language is no exception, it may be open to the teacher of religion to examine religious statements in terms of the period in which they were made. There need be no indoctrination in this, nor would such treatment be anti-religious. The teacher could be objective yet sympathetic, conveying the attitude that man's attempt to answer ultimate questions is valuable regardless of divergent answers.

Paul Tillich (1964, pp. 146-57) provides an interesting insight into this kind of approach. He argues that the school has two functions which he calls the 'inducting' and the 'humanistic'. The school has to 'induct' children into sets of symbols; it also has to develop their human potential. When the school is unduly concerned with the former function, the minds of the children are imposed on. Yet it is a necessary part of schooling. Tillich argues, then, that with these distinctions in mind, religious education becomes possible and justifiable. The teacher of religion must recognize that the symbols are responses to *real* questions, which *real* men have asked. To try, however, to give the pupils answers to questions they do not want to ask or do not see the point of, is to bore them. When the questions do arise the answers can be given in terms of the religious symbols which must then be reinterpreted in the light of the original question. That is, the religious answers will be given but not as final answers: 'The humanistic question is radical; it goes to the roots and does not accept anything whatever as being beyond question' (p. 154). Secondly, the school must lead the pupil to penetrate the symbols for the conceptual interpretation which lies beneath them. This does not imply, for Tillich, delaying the teaching of the symbols until the child can understand them: to do this would prevent any full experience of their power later.

From the existential theologian to the analytic philosopher may seem a mighty leap but in terms of our present concern it is worth making. As I have already mentioned, some modern philosophers have argued that religious statements are not real statements at all. They are unverifiable and hence 'meaningless': they are neither true nor false (Ayer, 1946, ch. 6). This view has been widely debated and few philosophers now accept it in this extreme form. But as I have shown, the controversy has focused attention on the precise nature and function of religious language.

This suggests that one form of religious education might consist in the analysis of theological statements and the elucidation of religious concepts. Cunningham (1957) has suggested that this manner of 'teaching religion' would be appropriate even in the American public schools since neutrality is in no way prejudiced by such treatment. Phenix (1955) proposes a similar solution: the schools should explore the philosophic issues characteristic of religious inquiry without preaching any dogmas. Such suggestions are scorned by many religionists in that this is not 'teaching religion' and is not neutral either since it is biased in favour of those who hold religious phenomena to be purely natural. While these replies have some validity they seem prejudicial to any attempt to solve the indoctrination problem. If a real problem does exist, as I have argued it does, sincere people must attempt to wrestle with the issue rather than retreat into opposing blocs.

Religion as verifiable

Some contemporary theologians and philosophers have

argued that while theological statements are really cognitive (i.e. they do say something), they refer not to a supernatural world but to the natural world. They are statements about man and his search for meaning. These writers draw attention to Jesus as an historical personality and to the Gospels as existing documents. Statements about them are meaningful and verifiable: faith comes in when one takes a stand towards the life and message of Jesus.

Van Buren (1965) has himself proposed a method for teaching religion in accordance with his views. The religious educator, he claims, has three tasks today: (i) to tell the Christian story as a story; (ii) to clarify the relationship between faith and knowledge; and (iii) to clarify the relationship between believing and living.

The first is a simple and acceptable procedure. Children love stories, and the religious heritage is full of stories. There can be no objection to telling children such stories. The problem arises when children ask as they do ask, did it really happen? At this point, the teacher's own beliefs will tend to intrude and indoctrination becomes a real danger. The wife of the Bishop of Woolwich makes the point that the task of the parent is to make clear the distinction between the historical fact ('Jesus was born in Bethlehem') and the interpretation believers place on it (Ruth Robinson, 1965, p. 126). Mrs Robinson's practical suggestions are of interest as she is representative of those parents who try to be honest with their children about religion and yet do not want to deprive them of a form of life which has nourished their own development. With her, as with most of the others, however, the danger of indoctrination is rarely of concern: there is talk of honesty, freedom, and authenticity, but a peculiar blindness to the issue of indoctrination and the injustice involved in indoctrinating the minds of the children with beliefs which are doubtful as distinct from those which the parent believes are doubtful. That is to say, when one considers the indoctrination problem as central it is clear that the issue is not how liberal or traditional the parent is in his belief. For if the child is rigorous in the way he holds religious propositions to be mythological, or in the way he holds them to be scientific, he has been indoctrinated equally; for each is an interpretation which is open to question. If the story approach is followed, questions about their status must be answered in terms of the real doubt that exists.

To clarify the relationship between faith and knowledge, as Van Buren suggests, would seem no easy task. Van Buren likens such teaching to teaching about love. One can point to exemplars of love and discuss it; loving is something more. Van Buren does not continue the parallel further, but it would be safe to say that children learn love by experience and imitation. Probably they learn faith in the same way but there is a problem here which was raised in a reply to van Buren. Ramsey held that in addition to teaching about faith and its relation to reason, one has to teach about him to whom the affirmation is made. Objectivity of some sort is needed or else the act of faith is an irrational gesture (Ramsey, 1965). This is very relevant to our present concern since there is the obvious danger of indoctrination in a particular view of Christ. Perhaps the most that a conscientious teacher could do would be to demonstrate by means of stories what faith has meant to others such as the disciples, the early Christians, the saints, and contemporary men.

The relationship between belief and action raises similar problems. The safest procedure might be to discuss the commitment others have supported by faith in Christ. The honest teacher would at the same time show that men of other faiths and none have done similar things, with different justification, and that Christians in the name of their God have performed deeds deserving of contempt. Conclusions as to what can be said about the relationship between belief and action can be left to the students as ultimately they must be in any system of education.

The suggestions given above for possible approaches to the teaching of religion are, of course, extremely vague. If any of them were to find acceptance by teachers of religion they would have to be spelled out and translated into a curriculum of some sort. The main significance of this sketchy account as I see it is: (i) once the problem of indoctrination is grasped (and it is amazing how few believers seem able to grasp it), new light is thrown on the whole task of religious education; (ii) the account does bring home the fact that it is not necessarily an either/or matter: either we indoctrinate or we leave children totally illiterate in one area of human concern. Educational solutions are feasible.

This can be taken as support for the importance of conceptual clarity in educational matters. When we have made some conceptual distinctions (in this case, between 'education' and 'indoctrination') we are better able to make rational decisions about curriculum and method. The distinction between education and indoctrination opens up a whole new way for evaluating programmes of instruction in most curricular areas but especially in politics, morals, and religion. I have concentrated on the religious side, but have also indicated the way in which thinking might move in the teaching of morals and politics. As with everything said in this book, counter-arguments are possible. People

may argue against my analysis of 'indoctrination' or produce good reasons for thinking that, say, morals or religion
are not the sorts of things in which the concept is of
concern. So be it. I will have succeeded in sparking off a
discussion and that in itself, I believe, is a contribution to
the education of the reader.

Religion and habits

The suggestions which have been given presume that the
child is of an age where abstract ideas and ideals, rational
justifications, and historical and theological concerns can be
appreciated and discussed. Some of the methods suggested
imply in fact that the child has passed from Piaget's stage
of concrete operations to that of formal operations, and
almost all require some degree of rational sophistication.

We now have to direct our concern to those early years
in which rational education is not possible. Habit and
training mark, and must mark, the early years of the
child's life. We must ask ourselves what can be legitimately done in these years for the religious training of the
child.

Since we have been concerned in this book with
indoctrination which, I have argued, is concerned with
beliefs, the emphasis has been on the cognitive side of
religion: the beliefs which are proposed for acceptance.
There is, of course, another side to religion. Religion is
regarded not only as a set of beliefs but as a way of life.
Some have regarded this as the real essence of religion:
Dewey, for example, eschewed 'religion' but supported
the 'religious'. Religion becomes merely an attitude of
reverence towards the world, and an appreciation of life's
mysteries. John Wilson (1970) argues that religion is

primarily concerned with *emotions* (e.g. awe and love of God, guilt for sin, reverence for the Buddha, and so on). Wilson and his associates are hoping to develop methods of teaching religion which take account of the emotional quality of religious thinking as distinct from the predominantly cognitive nature of their work on morality.

In asking what can be legitimately done by way of early training we need to remind ourselves that this is intimately tied up with the objective status of what it is proposed to impart. Where there is an area of knowledge which is in fact firmly based, we need have no hesitation at all in inducting children into it as soon as we think it necessary and have good reason for believing that they can cope with it. Mathematics and science are examples of this kind of knowledge. Since these are not matters of general dispute, we are not in very much danger of violating the child's rationality even if we have to present the ideas in greatly simplified or even distorted form.

At the opposite pole, where there are no good grounds for thinking that any of the beliefs are true, we have no warrant for teaching them at all. Astrology, animism, and witchcraft fall into this category and we would not regard it as legitimate to introduce children to these beliefs and practices.

Midway stand those matters on which there are no universally accepted standards or facts but where there are some more or less rational procedures in accordance with which people can form or modify their ideas and engage in dispute with others. Morals, etiquette, and politics belong in this category. In these areas the educator faces his principal problems. For we have good reason to believe that unless particular habits and attitudes are instilled in the early years, there is every likelihood that totally

93

unplanned habits and attitudes will develop. If no table manners are instilled, the child will habitually disregard all such niceties. He will tend to reject etiquette itself rather than a particular rule of etiquette. (See the earlier section on negative education, p. 69.) On the other hand we know that very often habits and attitudes which are stamped in during the early years persist in rigid form into adult life.

Faced with this dilemma, the best that the educator can do is to ensure that (i) the methods he uses are morally defensible—torture, savage punishment, and persistent conditioning are ruled out; (ii) the 'content' is in line with the best thinking available; in morality, for example, the moral principles taught should be universalizable and related to the feelings of other people rather than narrow, specific, and egocentric; and (iii) the 'content' should be presented in such a way as to encourage the child to develop a critical spirit towards it.

When we turn our attention to religious practices, we find that many people talk and act as if religion falls into the first category. They argue that just as we simplify science to teach the young, so we are entitled to simplify theology and instil particular religious attitudes and habits. On this view, there are no specific limits on what can be taught and how it can be taught. I hope I have said enough in earlier sections to indicate the deficiency of this position.

Others seem to suggest that religion is more like astrology and witchcraft. It is false and misguided and there is no excuse for teaching it at all. This viewpoint assumes for atheism a truth value similar to science and consequently is no more defensible than the previous position which asserts that theism is of the same order as a scientific discipline.

94

Religion, then, must be treated like morality. There are some rational procedures although these are limited and an uncomfortable degree of subjectivity remains. Among sophisticated people, rational dialogue on religion is possible. The aim of the religious educator is to prepare the child to enter into that dialogue, if not with others then at least with himself.

The early years of a child's life are marked more by informal and formal introduction to a way of life than by rational dialogue on abstract issues. In matters of religion much of this is done by means of prayer, religious objects, grace at meals, Bible-reading, church attendance. For those who incline towards atheistic, agnostic, or humanistic ways of life, training may involve poetry, nature study, and habituation in concern for one's fellow man.

Since a way of life is caught as much as taught, it would be futile as well as presumptuous to suggest that a parent train a child to a way of life he himself does not follow. For the essence of training lies in consistency, and the parent's own outlook has to be part of this consistency. That is to say, it must be obvious that a Catholic parent can only induct into a Catholic way of life, a Jewish parent into a Jewish, an atheist into an atheistic; to me this seems not a prescription but an empirical reality. Delaying such training will not serve, for patterns of behaviour are set down very early, and to refuse to enforce any patterns is to condition to another way of life, not to none. If *some* kind of religious outlook (broadly construed) is desirable, a *particular* one has to be built in during the child's early years.

As in all forms of early training, however, there are limits to what can be done and it is necessary to suggest tentatively some of these limits.

1   The religious training of whatever variety should be seen as placing the child in the way of experiences upon which religious education, not religious indoctrination, can be built. The explanations which accompany the religious practices must obey the rules for cognitive training: uncertainty must be conveyed as soon as it becomes relevant to do so.

2   The age of the child must be taken into account. What is justifiable for the three-year-old is not justifiable for the teenager. As the child grows older, impositions of religious practice should steadily decrease and opportunities be given for him to come in contact with other ways of life. Religious education, like moral education, begins when the child perceives the possibility of choice.

3   The means should be morally acceptable. Just as extreme anxiety, fear, and the withdrawal of the parents' love are unacceptable means of social training, so reliance on hell-fire, the withdrawal of God's love, and preoccupation with death are objectionable means of religious training.

If these rather general principles are translated into a programme, the danger of religious indoctrination should be minimized. It is encouraging to find among recent writers on religious education a growing awareness of the issue of indoctrination. (For a review of some of the recent literature, see Hull, 1970.) A splendid example of this development, coupled with an awareness of the distinction between habit-formation and indoctrination is provided by the following extract:

Education has become a matter of investigation rather than indoctrination. To regard religious education as aiming at conversion is to prevent its being influenced

by this educational advance, and to base it on ecclesias-
tical rather than educational principles. It may possibly
be argued that the subject cannot be treated in the same
way as others, since the ideas it attempts to convey are
not susceptible to the empirical verification that is
available in physics and mathematics. Religion, it is
said, is not a matter that children can comprehend by
investigation. It needs wider experience than they can
bring to it and involves problems which even adults
can answer only by recourse to revealed authority
or faith. Yet children need some guidance in religion
and must be given authoritative guidance in it just as
they are given authoritative guidance on going to the
dentist or how to behave at table. One suspects that
there is a confusion of thought here between ideas and
actions. The statement that children need guidance in
religion is an indirect way of saying that the virtue of
religion is its good effect on conduct and that children
should be directed to behave in a Christian manner. But
while it may be permissible to give guidance on how to
behave to children who have not yet the experience and
insight to appreciate the implications of their actions,
is it educationally sound, or even possible, to tell them
what they are to think or believe? Is not this to give
them adult ideas, which they cannot assimilate, but
will hold as verbalisms to be repeated at appropriate
occasions without being understood? It would seem
more realistic to regard training in religious ideas as
educationally similar to those of other subjects, basing
them on the children's interpretation of experience, thus
making them more genuine if less extensive. [Cox, 1966,
pp. 63-4.]

Conclusion

In this chapter the discussion of indoctrination has been

related to morals, politics, and religion. It was suggested that with thought and care programmes of moral, political, and religious education may be possible. In order to exemplify this view, some possible approaches to religious education were outlined. It is important to realize that each is very tentative and all are open to indoctrinatory techniques. The key factor, it must be stressed, is the agent's intention. If he intends to educate rather than indoctrinate, such methods may enable him to carry out his intentions. If he intends fixed beliefs, he can readily use these methods to indoctrinatory effect: no method, of itself, can prevent indoctrination. This has been the force of the argument in previous chapters and it bears repeating.

Early education has been considered and limited approval given to some training of the very young in religion. This training is to be deplored if (i) immoral means are used, or (ii) the intention is bad, or (iii) it is very intensive and unduly limiting on freedom, or (iv) it is combined with, or used to prepare for, indoctrination.

Throughout this chapter and in previous chapters 'indoctrination' has been contrasted with 'education' and there has been no real attempt to justify this distinction. Other terms such as 'conditioning', 'teaching', and 'brainwashing' have also been used in the argument with very little elucidation. In the final chapter 'indoctrination' will be related to these other terms. The purpose of this is (i) to make one final attempt at showing what indoctrination is, and (ii) to indicate that the terms can function in a consistent and useful way in educational theory.

5

Indoctrination and other concepts

The principal purpose of analysis is to make distinctions which for a particular purpose seem worth making. Analysis of educational concepts finds its warrant in the realization of conceptual distinctions which are of value to the educational theorist and to the practising teacher. The principal terms around which educational prescription revolves are 'education', 'indoctrination', and 'teaching'. It is important that these terms be clearly distinguished and their relationship to each other indicated in a coherent manner. This book has centred on 'indoctrination' and a work of at least equal length would be required to elucidate the others. It is not possible to discuss the other key terms in anything like the manner in which the term 'indoctrination' has been discussed. Nevertheless, what can be done is to show that this analysis can be made consistent with analyses of the other concepts. The suggestion is that the usefulness of this analyis is enhanced if it can be shown that it can fit into the general framework in which educational theory must operate. Consequently, in this chapter the terms 'education' and 'teaching' will be discussed briefly.

Another way of highlighting the analysis of 'indoctrination' is to relate it to other terms to which it has affinity, not because they are important in education but because they share its connotation of being dubious ways of influencing people. This chapter will deal with 'conditioning', 'progaganda', and 'brainwashing'. Indoctrination is often confused with these and some attempt, however insufficient, should be made to sort out some differences.

Teaching

Some writers have written into the concept of 'teaching' severe restrictions of manner. Thus teaching is seen as one sort of process and indoctrination, conditioning, and persuading are processes which are not teaching but are similar to it in some respects. In a well-known article, Green speaks of the 'contrast between teaching and indoctrination' (Green, 1964-5, p. 43) and many other analyses of 'teaching' draw similar distinctions. This stipulation flies in the face of ordinary usage which is not so restrictive. We speak of teaching someone to ride a bicycle and there is no suggestion of verbal instruction. We teach little children to talk or draw and there is no suggestion of giving reasons. We teach older students facts about geography and we do not imply that the evidence for these facts is given.

It might be argued that although the term 'teaching' does not entail procedural restrictions, more is logically involved than the intention that someone should learn. In a book in the same series as this monograph, it is argued that two other conditions are required: (i) that the teaching activities involve some display of what is to be learned, (ii) that the material be intelligible to the learner (Hirst and Peters, 1970, pp. 79-81).

I am inclined to say that these criteria are adequately

covered by the concept of 'intention', which suggests some connection between what one is doing and what one is intending. I cannot intend to chop down a tree with a rubber axe or intend to destroy the moon just by thinking about it. Wishes and wants, desires and dreams do not constitute intentions.

Both these positions have their problems. On my account, a person cannot intend to do something which cannot be done, even if he thinks it can be done, which seems to go against our usage (see Meiland, 1970, pp. 43-7). On the alternative view, many contingent matters (e.g. a healthy pupil, adequate light) get sucked into the *concept* of 'teaching'. Faced with this dilemma, I prefer to restrict analysis to the intention that someone learn and leave the other criteria contingently connected to intentions of certain sorts.

Granted that 'teaching' is a general concept, there are distinctions which are germane to the issue of indoctrination. We speak of teaching someone *to* do something, where the element of skill is stressed and we speak of teaching *that* something is the case where factual or theoretical knowledge is uppermost. 'Indoctrination' is concerned with the second of these: it is relevant where beliefs rather than skills are the desired outcome. When we wish to cast some aspersion on the teaching of skills, we use the term 'conditioning'.

While the term 'teach' can refer to any attempt to foster learning, there is a narrower use which implies that the agent not only *tries* to secure learning but assumes some responsibility for seeing that he has some success. The teacher becomes an authority figure and his performance is extended over a period of time. I have argued that 'indoctrination' is linked to this concept of teaching. Only a person in an authority role can indoctrinate and the statement 'you cannot indoctrinate in half an hour' is a conceptual truth.

All cases of indoctrination are cases of teaching. To say that someone is indoctrinating is not to deny that he is teaching; it is to presuppose that he is. Some sorts of teaching cannot be cases of indoctrination: only where beliefs are being imparted is 'indoctrination' appropriate. Finally, indoctrination suggests that the person so accused is a teacher in a more than minimal sense: he has assumed responsibility for learning. The point of the criticism is that he has violated his trust.

Education

R. S. Peters has argued that 'education' always implies a judgment of value. Whenever we call a process education, we express our approval of what is being passed on and the manner of its transmission. Taken as a tight conceptual point, this view has been shown to be defective. As a consequence, in a more recent paper (Peters, 1970) Peters has argued for two concepts—one in which the value component is necessarily implied and one in which it is not.

The literature growing up around the concept of education is of great interest and there are conceptual points of some complexity involved. For our purposes it is not necessary to enter fully into this debate. For, as we have seen in our discussion of 'indoctrination', the chances of producing a totally watertight analysis are remote. An analysis of strong plausibility is as much as can be hoped for.

Looked at in this way, Peters' analysis is most useful. We do in fact tend to use the term 'education' in a favourable sense. To speak of someone as educated is normally to praise him. To call someone an educator is to commend his work. This is so true, that we rarely call ourselves educators since humility deters us from praising our own efforts. To say we are teachers is safer and more neutral.

That is to say, if any of the key educational terms carries notes of approval it is 'education'. 'Education' carries a plus sign where 'indoctrination' carries a minus sign. Neither stands for any particular process although each implies that teaching has occurred. 'Education' represents a favourable judgment on the teaching. 'Indoctrination' denotes an unfavourable judgment.

The contrast between these two terms can be further reduced by considering their achievement sense. To say that a man is educated is to express approval; to say he is indoctrinated is to condemn him. This approval or disapproval is connected not with the amount of knowledge he has but with the quality of it, the way it is organized, and the use he makes of it. Again Peters' analysis is instructive. An educated man possesses (i) a high degree of understanding: he is not simply trained and his responses are not drilled, (ii) a sense of commitment to this knowledge: he respects the evidence and conforms to the standards of disciplined inquiry, and (iii) a cognitive perspective: his knowledge is integrated in a conceptual scheme and there are no 'compartments' immune from scrutiny. By contrast, the indoctrinated person often tends to stock answers to difficult questions, is incompletely committed to the full ramifications of his knowledge and reserves to himself some area of knowledge which is rationally untouchable, immune to argument and logic.

'Teaching' then is the neutral term. Of it an appraisal can be made in terms of rational criteria. When this appraisal is favourable, the process is termed 'education' and its product an educated man. When it is unfavourable, the same teaching processes are called 'indoctrination' and the resultant product is called an indoctrinated man.

Conditioning

In discussions of 'indoctrination' it has become a convention to distinguish it from conditioning on the grounds that conditioning is concerned with behaviour and indoctrination with beliefs (see, for example, Wilson, 1967, p. 169). I myself subscribe to this distinction because (i) it is one which has its warrant in ordinary language and (ii) it is a useful distinction in discussing the education of the young child.

This simple-minded distinction, however, is not without its problems.

1 'Indoctrination' is a term of ordinary language; 'conditioning' is a technical term in psychology. Hamlyn (1970) has argued for an extremely purist concept of conditioning on the grounds that when it is extended even slightly it loses any of the explanatory power it might have had. He also argues that, even in psychology, it has been stretched so much that it serves no useful function. Watson (1970) in reply makes the point that the extension of a term can be useful in bringing some poorly understood phenomenon under a general rubric. The use of the term in ordinary language can, I think, be justified on similar grounds. To say that someone's behaviour has been conditioned is to say that although the behaviour may be rational the agent does not know that it is. He acts *because of* his training and not because of his perception of what he ought to do.

2   A strict behaviourist would say that the distinction between beliefs and behaviour cannot be sustained. 'Beliefs' are species of verbal behaviour and they arise from conditioning too. It can be seriously questioned whether beliefs can be explained in terms of conditioning, however loosely the term is used (see Langford, 1968, pp. 78-85). At any rate, we do draw a clear distinction between beliefs and behaviour, and this is sufficient to make the conditioning-indoctrination distinction.

The early training of the child is marked by the inculcation of certain habits and skills. It is not too imprecise to use the term 'conditioning' for this. Some forms of training resemble operant conditioning (the child is rewarded or punished for certain behaviour and his future behaviour is thereby shaped); others are more akin to classical conditioning (saying a prayer becomes associated with going to bed or eating a meal).

Since this conditioning process is necessary for the child's early upbringing it cannot be condemned. Nevertheless, 'conditioning' unlike 'teaching' is not a completely neutral term. We may speak quite happily of the conditioning of the infant but to say of an adult that his behaviour has been conditioned is to express a criticism. The idea seems to be that while conditioning may be acceptable as an expedient, it must soon yield to rational habits.

In terms of evaluative tone, then, 'conditioning' differs from 'teaching', 'education', and 'indoctrination'. Unlike 'teaching', it is not completely value-neutral. It entails elements of criticism since there is a general belief that processes which by-pass human rationality are less acceptable than rational activities. Unlike 'indoctrination', however, it is not always condemned. It is regarded as an acceptable method of training when rational methods are not possible, e.g. with very young children, the mentally subnormal, and those suffering from severe psychoses or neuroses. It differs from 'education' in that the latter suggests a process which is approved.

Conditioning can operate as a method of teaching where what is being taught is a matter of behaviour. It cannot be part of the process of education, since it lacks the element of wittingness on the part of the subject (Peters, 1966, p. 41). It can however be a prelude to education as has been mentioned in connection with moral and religious training. Equally, it can prepare for or accompany indoctrination. It is very often the case that conditioning is used to supplement indoctrination as when children are taught to salute a flag, spit on Jews, chant slogans, or show deference to a religious leader. When used in this way conditioning shares the odium of indoctrination.

Propaganda

Indoctrination is sometimes equated with propaganda. There are good reasons for this. They share a great deal: moral opprobrium, non-rational methods, illiberal aims, and a certain frame of mind as an outcome. It is useful to attempt to distinguish them although no perfect contrast can be sustained.

Propaganda is associated in many minds with the machinations of ruthless dictators seeking to gain or preserve power. But it is not restricted to such usage. In times of war, democratic nations resort to it, as do advertisers at the best of times. Much of this may be open to criticism but our dislike of the grosser forms ought not to dispose us to dismiss it, like indoctrination, as necessarily evil. A medical association may use propaganda to win support for some defensible programme which people will not yet accept on purely rational grounds. Propaganda may involve mere repetition of one view; it may, and often does, involve emotional appeals, misrepresentation, distortions, and lies. It is likely that even in a free society, propaganda of some sort is being continually used. As long as there is a place for all kinds of propaganda, we do not object too much. But when the propaganda is single-minded as in the case of a dictator, or when the type of propaganda is morally offensive, we take umbrage.

Indoctrination is more defined: it occurs when somebody takes advantage of a privileged role (a 'teaching' role of some sort) to implant certain beliefs. Although it is not just children who can be indoctrinated, the pupil-teacher, child-parent relationships do seem to provide the paradigm cases of it. It is probably very difficult to indoctrinate an adult without a good deal of further reinforcement: propaganda, censorship, brainwashing. To indoctrinate a child is pathetically easy as every educational theorist and social reformer has intuitively recognized. If one wants to say that a strong dictator, being a charismatic figure and controlling the media, is indoctrinating when he uses propaganda, that is acceptable. It merely shows that the two terms can coincide, not that they are synonymous.

Brainwashing

Brainwashing is a comparatively new term. Despite the emotions it arouses, it does not seem to refer to any new or mysterious process. Basically it involves the use of all known methods to change a person's pattern of thinking and feeling: conditioning, anxiety, fear, indoctrination, distortions, drugs, group analyses, enforced isolation—all are used in a massive attempt to change a person's outlook. That this method should be needed is testimony that once a person is an adult it is difficult to indoctrinate him although earlier indoctrination can be reinforced. It is strange that while most people can see the evil of brainwashing, that of indoctrination is less often recognized. Yet, the intention is similar and where successful the result is similar. The main difference is that one is a method needed for adults, the other is all that is required for immature children.

It follows that in discussing indoctrination two errors should be avoided: (i) the suggestion that in accusing someone of indoctrinating we are accusing him of the brutal methods sometimes used by brainwashers. This is not only unjust but subversive of the whole case. For he has merely to show how kindly he treated the children to rebut the charge. Indoctrinators do not normally use brainwashing techniques: they do not need to if they can influence the children when they are young. (ii) The implication that there is a vast moral gap between the two. There need not be. The evidence suggests that not all brainwashing is done by harsh and brutal means. Some prisoners are in fact brainwashed by humane methods. The *intention* is the key moral factor in such cases and it is little different from that of the indoctrinator.

Conclusion

The discerning reader will have noticed that running through the whole book has been a concern for human rationality. It is time to make this commitment explicit.

It seems to me that whenever a person sets out to educate he commits himself by that very fact to the importance of rationality. For what else could he mean by educating children other than to want them to know what is true rather than what is false and to do what is reasonable rather than what is unreasonable? The notion of setting out to make people irrational *in every way* seems unintelligible and certainly could not be called education. The case for rationality as the aim of education is *prima facie* established.

However, while it is difficult to believe that anyone could value irrationality completely there are positions which are intelligible and which might go some way towards attacking the point of view advanced in this book.

1 The objection might be raised that although rationality is important it is not the only value. Commitment, service, love of one's fellow man are equally to be esteemed and no educator can neglect these.

Nothing that has been said in these pages constitutes a denial of these values. Irrational commitment is fanaticism, and service and love not based on a correct analysis of the situation is mere maudlin sentiment. The emotions themselves unless they are to run riot are restrained by the cognitive: to take pride in what is not in any way the result of one's efforts is conceptually absurd; to love what is judged to be evil is a distortion of human emotion. Rationality does not impede emotion, love, and service. It is a necessary condition of them. The concern to avoid indoctrination is in no way inimical to the other virtues which educators may aim at. It merely places restrictions on how they are to be fostered.

2 Another argument might be that although rationality is by and large to be fostered, there are areas in which

the educator must not be concerned about it. For example, it might be argued that love of country precludes telling the whole truth; that in moral matters some cannot be allowed to think for themselves but must be taught (even, yes, indoctrinated) to follow the authority of those who know; that in religious matters, the human mind is imperfect and must bow to God's revelation.

There is not space to tackle these powerful objections here. It must suffice to make the following points:

i Whoever excludes from rational scrutiny any area of human concern takes upon himself a fearsome responsibility. He must face the lessons of history in which again and again we see truth, justice, and human dignity fall victim to this type of thinking. At the very least, such a position needs rational justification and those who are to be the victims or beneficiaries (depending on one's views) are, as rational agents, entitled to this justification.

ii That there are higher sources of knowledge than human reason is a claim made by humans: it is not a self-evident truth. Like any other empirical claim it requires evidence, backing, and sound reasoning. To indoctrinate this claim and then to deduce other claims from it is to reject man's basic claim to rational dignity. That these injustices have been perpetrated and continue to be perpetrated in the name of religion must indeed be one of the greatest indictments of religion and religious training.

The educator, whether he is a parent or a teacher, faces an awesome task. He must initiate immature minds into a cultural heritage, and train unformed consciences to know and love what is good. At the same time he is bound to respect the rationality, potential or actual, which these young people embody. No pedagogical trick, no psychological evidence, no amount of folk wisdom can tell him how to balance these difficult obligations. Yet balance them he must, and in order to do so he must relentlessly and painfully wrestle with the conceptual issues raised in this book.

Select bibliography

The following provide the 'main core' of contemporary discussions of indoctrination:

ATKINSON, R. F. (1965), 'Instruction and indoctrination' in Archambault, R. D. (ed.), *Philosophical Analysis and Education*. London: Routledge & Kegan Paul.

CRITTENDEN, BRIAN S. (1968), 'Teaching, educating, and indoctrinating', *Educational Theory*, 18, Summer 1968, 237-52.

FLEW, ANTONY (1966), 'What is indoctrination?', *Studies in Philosophy and Education*, IV, 3, Spring 1966, 281-306.

FLEW, ANTONY (1967), ' "What is indoctrination?" Comments on Moore and Wilson', *Studies in Philosophy and Education*, V, Spring 1967, 273-83.

GREGORY, I. M. M. and WOODS, R. G. (1970), 'Indoctrination', *Proceedings of the Annual Conference January 1970*, The Philosophy of Education Society of Great Britain, 77-105.

HARE, R. M. (1964), 'Adolescents into adults' in Hollins, T. H. B. (ed.), *Aims in Education: The Philosophic Approach*, Manchester: Manchester University Press.

MOORE, W. (1966), 'Indoctrination as a normative conception', *Studies in Philosophy and Education*, IV, Summer 1966, 396-403.

SNOOK, I. A. (1970), 'The concept of indoctrination', *Studies in Philosophy and Education*, VII, 2, Fall 1970, 65-108.

WHITE, J. P. (1967), 'Indoctrination', in Peters, R. S. (ed.), *The Concept of Education*, London: Routledge & Kegan Paul.

WHITE, J. P. (1970), 'Indoctrination: reply to I. M. M. Gregory and R. G. Woods', *Proceedings of the Annual Conference January 1970*, The Philosophy of Education Society of Great Britain, 107-20.

WILSON, J. (1964), 'Education and indoctrination' in Hollins, T. H. B. (ed.), *Aims in Education: The Philosophic Approach*, Manchester: Manchester University Press.

WILSON, J. (1966), 'Comment on Flew's "What is Indoctrination?"', *Studies in Philosophy and Education*, IV, Summer 1966, 390-5.

For a discussion of the related issue of 'neutrality' see:

ECKSTEIN, J. (1969), 'Is it possible for the schools to be neutral?' *Educational Theory*, 19:4, Fall 1969, 337-46.

ENNIS, R. H. (1959), 'The "impossibility" of neutrality', *Harvard Educational Review*, 29:2, 1959. Reprinted in Smith, B. O. and Ennis R. H. (eds.), *Language and Concepts in Education*, Chicago: Rand McNally 1961.

ENNIS, R. H. (1969), 'The possibility of neutrality', *Educational Theory*, 19:4, Fall 1969, 347-56.

FRENCH, E. L. (1963), *Melbourne Studies in Education*, Melbourne: Melbourne University Press. Five papers on 'Objectivity and neutrality in public education' (by E. L. French, D. P. Derham, D. H. Monro, E. J. Storman, and J. D. McCaughley).

HOFFMAN, D. C. (1964), 'The schools and neutrality: in response to Professor Robert H. Ennis', *Educational Theory*, 14:3, July 1964, 182-5.

MCCLELLAN, J. E. (1968), 'The politicizing of educational theory: a re-evaluation', *Philosophy of Education 1968*, Proceedings of the (American) Philosophy of Education Society.

Bibliography

A.A.U.P. Bulletin (1967), 'Academic freedom and tenure: Adelphi University', 53, September.

AYER, A. J. (1946), *Language, Truth and Logic*, New York: Dover.

BIDDLE, W. W. (1932), *Propaganda and Education*, New York: Teachers College Press.

BOWERS, C. A. (1969), *The Progressive Educator and the Depression: The Radical Years*, New York: Random House.

BRAITHWAITE, R. B. (1955), *An Empiricist's View of Religious Belief*, Cambridge: Cambridge University Press.

BRAMELD, T. (1956), *Toward a Reconstructed Philosophy of Education*, New York: Dryden Press.

BUREN VAN, P. M. (1965), 'Christian education *post-mortem dei*', *Religious Education*, 60, Jan.-Feb., 4-10.

CHOMSKY, N. (1959), Review of B. F. Skinner's *Verbal Behaviour* in *Language*, 35:1.

CORBETT, J. P. (1965), *Ideologies*, London: Hutchinson.

COULSON, C. A. (1966), *Science and Christian Belief*, London: Fontana.

COX, E. (1966), *Changing Aims in Religious Education*, London: Routledge & Kegan Paul.

CRITTENDEN, BRIAN S. (1968), 'Teaching, educating and indoctrinating', *Educational Theory*, 18, Summer, 237-52.

CUNNINGHAM, E. C. (1957), 'The logico-scientific status of selected theological concepts', *Educational Theory*, 7, April 1957, 81-92.

DUPUIS, A. and NORDBERG, R. (1964), *Philosophy and Educa-*

tion: A Total View, Milwaukee: Bruce.

ECKSTEIN, J. (1969), 'Is it possible for the schools to be neutral?' *Educational Theory*, 19:4, Fall, 337-46.

ELLUL, J. (1965), *Propaganda: The Formation of Men's Attitudes*, New York: Knopf.

ENNIS, R. H. (1959), 'The "impossibility" of neutrality', *Harvard Educational Review*, 29:2. Reprinted in B. O. Smith and R. H. Ennis (eds.), *Language and Concepts in Education*, Chicago: Rand McNally, 1961.

ENNIS, R. H. (1969), 'The possibility of neutrality', *Educational Theory*, 19:4, Fall, 347-56.

FLEW, ANTONY (1966), 'What is indoctrination?' *Studies in Philosophy and Education*, IV, 3, Spring, 281-306.

FLEW, ANTONY (1967), '"What is indoctrination?" Comments on Moore and Wilson', *Studies in Philosophy and Education*, V, 2, Spring, 273-83.

FLEW, A. and MACINTYRE, A. (1955), (eds.), *New Essays in Philosophical Theology*, London: SCM Press.

GATCHEL, RICHARD H. (1959), 'Evolution of concepts of indoctrination in American education', *Educational Forum*, 23, March, 303-9.

GREEN, T. F. (1964-5), 'A topology of the teaching concept', *Studies in Philosophy and Education*, III, Winter, 284-319.

GREGORY, I. M. M. and WOODS, R. G. (1970), 'Indoctrination', *Proceedings of the Annual Conference, January*, Philosophy of Education Society of Great Britain, 77-105.

GRIBBLE, J. (1969), *Introduction to Philosophy of Education*, Boston: Allyn and Bacon.

HAMLYN, D. W. (1970), 'Conditioning and Behaviour' in Borger, Robert and Cioffi, Frank (eds.), *Explanation in the Behavioural Sciences*, Cambridge: Cambridge University Press, 139-52.

HARE, R. M. (1964), 'Adolescents into adults' in Hollins, T. H. B. (ed.), *Aims in Education: The Philosophic Approach*, Manchester University Press.

BIBLIOGRAPHY

HEATER, D. B. (ed.) (1969), *The Teaching of Politics*, London: Methuen.

HESS, R. D. and TORNEY, J. V. (1968), *The Development of Political Attitudes in Children*, New York: Doubleday.

HICK, J. (1966), *Faith and Knowledge*, Ithaca, N.Y.: Cornell.

HIRST, P. H. (1966), 'Educational theory' in Tibble, J. W. (ed.), *The Study of Education*. London: Routledge & Kegan Paul.

HIRST, P. H. and PETERS, R. S. (1970), *The Logic of Education*, London: Routledge & Kegan Paul.

HOFFMAN, D. C. (1964), 'The schools and neutrality: in response to Professor Robert H. Ennis', *Educational Theory*, 14:3, July, 182-5.

HOLBROOK, C. A. (1963), *Religion: A Humanistic Field*, Englewood Cliffs: Prentice-Hall.

HULL, JOHN M. (1970), 'Recent developments in the philosophy of religious education', *Educational Review*, 23:1, November, 59-68.

HUNTER, E. (1956), *Brainwashing: from Pavlov to Powers*, New York: Bookmailer.

KILPATRICK, W. H. (1940), *Group Education for a Democracy*, New York: Association Press.

KILPATRICK, W. H. (1951), *Philosophy of Education*, New York: Macmillan.

KOHLBERG, L. (1963), 'The development of children's orientations towards a moral order', *Vita Humana*, 6, 11-33.

KOHLBERG, L. (1966), 'Moral education in the schools: a developmental view', *School Review*, 74, 1966, 1-30.

KOHLBERG, L. (1968), 'Education for justice: a modern statement of the Platonic view', Ernest Burton Lecture on Moral Education, Harvard University.

KOHLBERG, L. (1969), 'Stage and sequence: the cognitive developmental approach to socialization' in Goslin, D. (ed.), *Handbook of Socialization Theory and Research*, Chicago: Rand McNally.

116

LANGFORD, GLENN (1968), *Philosophy and Education*, London: Macmillan.

MACHAN, J. R. (1970), 'Education and the philosophy of knowledge', *Educational Theory*, 20, Summer.

MARTIN, JANE (1970), *Explaining, Understanding, and Teaching*, New York: McGraw-Hill.

MCCLELLAN, J. E. (1968), 'The politicizing of educational theory: a re-evaluation', *Philosophy of Education 1968*, Proceedings of the (American) Philosophy of Education Society.

MEILAND, JACK W. (1970), *The Nature of Intention*, London: Methuen.

MITCHELL, BASIL (1969), 'The Justification of Religious Belief' in High, Dallas M. (ed.), *New Essays in Religious Language*, New York: Oxford University Press, 178-97.

MOORE, W. (1966), 'Indoctrination as a normative conception', *Studies in Philosophy and Education*, Summer, 396-403.

NELL, O. (1969), 'Innocence and permissiveness', *Moral Education*, 1 : 3, December.

PASSMORE, J. (1967), 'On teaching to be critical' in Peters, R. S. (ed.), *The Concept of Education*, London: Routledge & Kegan Paul.

PETERS, R. S. (1966), *Ethics and Education*, London: Routledge & Kegan Paul.

PETERS, R. S. (1970), 'Education and the educated man', *Proceedings of the Annual Conference, 1970*, The Philosophy of Education Society of Great Britain, 5-20.

PHENIX, P. (1955), 'Religion in American public education', *Teachers College Record*, 57, October, 26-31.

RAMSEY, I. T. (1957), *Religious Language*, London: SCM Press.

RAMSEY, I. T. (1965), 'Discernment, commitment, and cosmic disclosure', *Religious Education*, 60, 1965.

ROBINSON, J. A. T. (1965), *The New Reformation*, Philadelphia: Westminster.

ROBINSON, RUTH (1965), 'Spiritual education in a world without religion', Appendix to Robinson, J. A. T., *The New Reformation.*

SARGANT, W. (1957), *Battle for the Mind*, Garden City, N.Y.: Doubleday.

SCHEFFLER, I. (1960), *The Language of Education*, Springfield, Ill.: Charles C. Thomas.

SCHEFFLER, I. (1965), *Conditions of Knowledge: An Introduction to Epistemology and Education*, Chicago: Scott, Foresman.

STANLEY, W. O. (1953), *Education and Social Integration*, New York: Teachers' College Press.

TILLICH, P. (1964), *Theology of Culture*, ed. R. C. Kimball, New York: Oxford University Press.

WATSON, A. J. (1970), 'Comment' in Borger, Robert, and Cioffi, Frank (eds.), *Explanation in the Behavioural Sciences*, Cambridge: Cambridge University Press, 153-61.

WHITE, J. P. (1967), 'Indoctrination' in Peters, R. S. (ed.), *The Concept of Education*, London: Routledge & Kegan Paul.

WHITE, J. P. (1970), 'Indoctrination: Reply to I. M. M. Gregory and R. G. Woods', *Proceedings of the Annual Conference, January*. The Philosophy of Education Society of Great Britain, 107-20.

WILSON, J. (1964), 'Education and indoctrination' in Hollins, T. H. B. (ed.), *Aims in Education: The Philosophic Approach*, Manchester: Manchester University Press.

WILSON, J. (1966), 'Comment on Flew's "What is indoctrination?"' *Studies in Philosophy and Education*, IV, Summer 1966, 390-5.

WILSON, J., WILLIAMS, N., SUGARMAN, B. (1967), *Introduction to Moral Education*, Harmondsworth: Penguin.

WILSON, J. (1970), *Approach to Religious Education*, Oxford: Farmington Trust.